VERMONT for Every Season

VERMONT
for Every Season

VERMONT LIFE MAGAZINE / MONTPELIER, VERMONT

Published by *Vermont Life* Magazine, 61 Elm Street, Montpelier, Vermont 05602, this book has been printed and bound in the United States of America.

Edited by Brian Vachon
Designed by Linda Dean Paradee

FIRST EDITION: October 1980

Library of Congress Cataloging in Publication Data
Main entry under title:

Vermont for every season

   1. Vermont—Description and travel—1951   —Ad-
dresses, essays, lectures. 2. Vermont—Social life
and customs—Addresses, essays, lectures. 1. Vachon,
Brian, 1941-
F55.V47   974.3   80-23320
ISBN 0-936896-00-0

Photograph opposite title page: Autumn in Peacham by Richard W. Brown

Contents

Introduction

Vermont is a constant marvel of new discoveries. That is why I enjoy living here. Vermont is good for my education.

But to be truthful, the discoveries I make are mostly *re*discoveries of what I knew but allowed to slip from memory. Take autumn as an example. Together with Reeve Brown, who contributes the essay entitled "Days of Splendor" to this volume, I am annually amazed by the phenomenon of brilliant foliage in early October. "Each year it takes us by surprise," she writes, and I share her feeling: "Each year we are caught unprepared and disbelieving until faced with the full-blown, indisputable spectacle of Vermont foliage. We had completely forgotten it was this lovely."

The yearly cycle in Vermont is a refresher course. It gets us "back to the basics"—the true basics about humankind being part of the natural world and the turning seasons of the changing calendar. And this volume is my textbook to remind me of what I knew once—and thought I knew forever.

No, this is not a textbook in the traditional sense. We can all be grateful for that. This book is too lively, too evocative for a label which implies a dull compendium, a recitation of facts. Nor do I suggest that immersing yourself in this volume is like enrolling in a classroom course with didactic professors lecturing at you, notes to be duly taken, and worrisome exams to prepare for. This book, like Vermont itself, is to be enjoyed. It shares with you the new discoveries which Vermonters make annually as the earth turns on its axis and reveals its marvels for all who care to enrich their lives.

That includes almost all the people who choose to live in Vermont. We number only 500,000 in a nation which now counts 215,000,000 residents. That stark statistic is a mind stopper: ask 215 Americans picked at random where they live and 214 of them will probably give an address outside of Vermont. (You can guess beforehand which one is the Vermonter by the puckish smile playing at the corners of the mouth and the quiet pride in the steady voice which declares "Vermont.")

But we don't mind being the third smallest state, in population, among all fifty states. Should Alaska and Wyoming exceed us in growth we would congratulate them cheerfully. Nor do we mind being the most rural state in the nation. Secretly, some of us regret that Vermont has grown to pass the half-million mark. While we appreciate the urban amenities which ease our lives, we still can look back nostalgically to an era which ended less than two decades ago, when Vermont had more cows than people. That ratio meant more Vermonters were in closer touch with the elemental verities of life—those "basics" that humankind needs to rediscover.

Fortunately, for many of us, that primal relationship is still a condition of our daily lives. In 1979 the 500,000 people of Vermont consumed 400,000 cords of firewood, and most of this timber was cut by Vermonters in Vermont. That is the highest per capita use of wood for heat in the United States. Vermont leads the nation in non-oil energy use. In 1980 and beyond it will be possible for Vermont to consume up to five million cords annually of home-grown firewood. Our forest resources are plentiful: we can get that much more wood energy from our standing timber without denuding our handsome landscape of its beautiful trees. Does that tell you something significant about how Vermonters relate their indoor lives with the world outdoors, with the rhythm of the seasons? Let your nose provide the answer: like John Vachon and other essayists in this book, you can smell the fragrant woodsmoke as it wafts from chimneys and flues. Use your eyes, too: notice the well-stacked woodpiles beside our homes. Sixty percent of all Vermont homeowners use wood for heat; twenty percent of all households use wood exclusively for heat.

Donna Fitch, who lives in a farmhouse in tiny Calais, north of Montpelier, and provides the essay on the harvest season for this volume, states this bond concisely: "It's the feeling of being connected with the land, with our neighbors, with our family, with Vermont," she writes. "It's a sensation we might call 'being one with nature,' or with God. It's the awareness of our continuity with the seasons. The importance, and yet the simplicity of our lives. The poignant feeling of beginnings and endings, and how one flows to and through another. We almost catch a glimpse of the 'why' of things."

Even in Burlington—large, sprawling Burlington, a metropolis by Vermont standards—this awareness can be detected. (Burlington must be viewed in context: no other state in the nation has as its largest community a city as small as Burlington. Take your bows, Cheyenne, Wyoming, and Anchorage, Alaska.) "It is a misconception," says Ralph Nading Hill, author of "Days to Celebrate" in this volume, "that the mystique that surrounds the traditional Christmas in a rural setting has escaped those of us born and raised even in the state's largest city, with Lake Champlain at its doorstep and Mount Mansfield and Camel's Hump in its backyard. The same snow, though somewhat less of it, that blankets the mountains covers Burlington, and many of the same influences and associations affecting the rest of the state have always drifted into the lives of its people."

In spirit, Vermonters are small-town people—even if some of our communities have increased dramatically and others are too minute to qualify even as hamlets. We are villagers at heart. Ralph Nading Hill also describes the mentality which pervades Vermont: "Instead of people predominating over the environment, the surroundings prevail and human individuality is magnified against them." In essence, he says, "Life in the Green Mountains guarantees an affinity with nature."

That is the theme of this book: Vermonters share "an affinity with nature." And we enjoy it, too.

"How so?" I hear a skeptic asking scornfully. "Enjoy it?" The voice is incredulous.

I have a fantasy—a nightmare, actually—in which an angry out-of-stater appears on my doorstep in Montpelier, a copy of this book under his arm, while a blizzard swirls the snow behind him, and howling winds are blowing razor-sharp out of the north, and the temperature drops down-down-down to the bottom of the thermometer. "You enjoy storms like this?" he asks sarcastically. "After this I suppose you like getting your car stuck in muck on dirt roads during mud season? And then the unexpected frost which nips your freshly planted garden? You *Vermont Life* writers are romantics. If Mount Mansfield erupted as a fiery volcano, and buried Stowe in molten lava, *Vermont Life* would describe the occurrence as the latest reason why tourists should go to Stowe. What human individuality exists in a driving snowstorm when a walker fades from sight only a few feet away, and a person's footprints are obliterated almost instantly?" He waves this book at the drifting snow behind him. "No wonder only 500,000 people live in Vermont. One of the constant marvels of Vermont is that 500,000 people *do* live here."

My fantasy-nightmare always catches me unprepared. Humbly, I thought this visitor was calling simply to ask me to autograph this beautiful book. By now I'm getting cold. An open doorway in a Vermont snowstorm is no place to achieve "an affinity with nature." I invite this critic inside. That *is* one of the constant marvels of Vermont: we're still innocent of big-city suspicions and treat strangers kindly.

My fantasy is no longer a nightmare. I tell my derisive guest how he should dress warmly in a Vermont winter—an elementary fact of life which many out-of-staters seem to have a hard time comprehending. I tell him how promptly the roads will be cleared by our efficient snow-removal crew; Montpelier, like Washington, D.C., is a capital city, but Montpelier, unlike Washington, doesn't lie prostrate after a snowstorm and react to it like a nuclear wipe-out. Individuality is expressed gratefully on skis *after* the storm is over, I tell my detractor; there is a distinction between human individuality and stupidity. I remind him that Vermonters know winter is inevitable. I refer him to the selection by John Vachon in the book he is carrying, and I point to the segment which says, "Vermonters await winter calmly, and with no trepidation. They've handled it before."

And if Mount Mansfield erupted as a volcano, and poured molten lava on Stowe, *Vermont Life* would probably describe the lava as an alternative source of heat for dealing with the energy crisis. I can picture some innovative Vermonters tapping the lava the same way we tap maple trees. I can even visualize the caption for such a scene in *Vermont Life:* "Vermonters still practice Yankee ingenuity in Stowe—a town which now exceeds ancient Pompeii as a mecca for tourists who want to see how life was quaintly lived before Mount Mansfield outdid Vesuvius as a volcano."

I'm putting you on: there are no volcanoes in Vermont. Besides, hot lava isn't allowed to flow unless first it is licensed under Vermont's very strict environmental laws.

But the climate in Vermont *is* extravagant—to use an adjective which recurs in Reeve Brown's essay. Zephine Humphrey, the famous writer who lived in Manchester, put this truth very aptly more than a half-century ago: weather she termed "an epic affair, deserving capital letters—WEATHER." The key to understanding the seasons in Vermont is to accommodate yourself to epic living.

Vermonters have been known to pick violets from snow-bare ground in December, and watch a snowstorm weigh down the branches of their budding rose bushes in June. They have seen rain fall in their front yards while sunshine bathed their backyards. Sunbathers in spring can get a chill and a burn at the same time. That is epic living.

But pleasure comes with adjusting to the capriciousness. I belong to a hunting lodge in North Fayston called "Sharpshooters," and our big event each year is a corn roast when the shocks are perfect for picking. But that's the riddle: we never know exactly when the corn will be ripe. As a consequence our corn roast is a movable feast which can be scheduled on short notice any time between mid-August and the hazy days after Labor Day weekend. As I write this Introduction the Christmas of 1979 is totally snowless; it looks like mud season outside. But while eating Easter dinner in 1978 at Elizabeth Dodge's home in Berlin the thick snow fell incessantly on Liz's spruce trees like the scene on a Christmas card. As a historian I have tried to analyze this erratic climate since observations were first recorded by the early Vermont settlers, but Lewis Hill of North Greensboro has written how this task is fruitless. "About twenty years ago I began keeping a daily record of weather and temperature," he confesses. "Now, after two decades, all I really know for sure is that New England weather is cussedly unpredictable, which any Yankee could have told me in the first place."

As a historian I also try to incorporate Vermont WEATHER into my professional life. Vermonters won the Battle of Bennington in 1777, the history books tell us, because a summer thunderstorm caused the advancing Hessian mercenaries to mire in the mud and be delayed by high water in the Battenkill. I can believe that. But the Vermont Constitution was ratified at Windsor on July 7, 1777, the history books tell us, because dissidents were forced by a sudden downpour to stay inside a tavern and resolve their discord instead of adjourning as scheduled and leaving their differences unsettled. I've often wondered about that. Vermonters are so familiar with thunderstorms it is hard to believe that one could intimidate the founders of our state.

I've also wondered if it is true, as residents of Pomfret claimed in 1775, that they could hear the sound of the echoing cannon being fired during the Battle of Bunker Hill, near Boston, about 110 air-miles away. And how about the residents of Craftsbury in 1814 who claimed they could hear the booming cannon fired during the Battle of Plattsburg across Lake Champlain? Both Pomfret and Craftsbury are hill towns; were the winds blowing in the right directions on those two fateful days? Did Vermonters, because of their reputations for taciturnity, have better ears in the pre-rock-and-roll era?

As a Vermont historian who collects specimens of Vermont humor, it seems to me that our native wit thrives on understated anecdotes, some so subtle and dry we watch out-of-staters carefully to see if they understand the drollery. But WEATHER is the single phenomenon in our daily lives which causes us to exaggerate—often to Texas-size proportions. The time-worn definition of our WEATHER in Vermont is "nine months of winter and three months of hard sledding." Other examples abound, such as the exchange between a tourist driving through Williamstown Gulf in June who encounters a Vermonter shoveling snow. Says the tourist:

"You must have had lots of snow here last winter." Replies the Vermonter:

"Oh no. This snow is from the winter before last."

Or Arthur Wallace Peach's tall tale about our thick cocoons of morning mist in the spring. One morning Peach, who was Director of the Vermont Historical Society, met a fisherman with a fine catch of bass near a mist-enshrouded stream in northern Vermont. The fisherman explained how he caught the bass:

"When the sun come up, I was sure stumped—I hadn't been fishing in the river at all. I had jist cast into the fog, an' them bass was swimmin' round in it, catching mosquitoes!"

There are exceptions, of course. Francis Colburn recalls Walter Wheeler of Craftsbury remarking one wet day, as the worst rainstorm in fifteen years pelted ferociously from the sky, "Well, Francis, it looks like rain, don't it?" At the height of the devastating hurricane of 1938 Walter was heard to observe: "God, it's airy, ain't it?"

Maybe Walter was putting Francis on.

That is one of the pleasures of accommodating to Vermont WEATHER. It is astounding how many people are still enthralled by the Vermont folktale, which first emerged from a pawky farmer named Allen Morse in Calais a century ago, telling how Vermonters freeze their old folks for the winter and then thaw them back to life in the spring. As a historian who aspires to be a ham actor (with apologies to pigs for maligning them by that insensitive use of "ham"), I hope some day to be as lucky as Bernard DeVoto, the widely read author whom Ralph Nading Hill mentions in his essay. DeVoto was about to lecture one night at the Bread Loaf Writers' Conference when an ominous thunderstorm descended on Ripton. Not to be upstaged by a rival act, DeVoto incorporated the storm into his presentation. He was speaking about religious fanatics in American history, and began by reading a passage from Isaiah about the end of the world—just as lightning and thunder shook the lecture room. When he characterized one group of religious zealots as being insane a door slammed in the gusty wind to punctuate his judgment. When he said they were hysterical the door slammed again. When he said they had failed in their mission the wind blew the door shut with a frightening crash. Mocking both his subject and the terrifying storm he said in the solemn, mournful voice of an Old Testament prophet: "These are troubled times." With that remark all the lights went out! He knew how to make history relevant to present conditions.

Accommodating to Vermont is a game of contrasts as well as handy juxtapositions. There is a farmer's field along Route 14 in East Montpelier which is gloriously yellow-bright with dandelions in May, but in winter, when I drive past it, it continually glows in my memory even when the contoured snow is neatly sculpted across it. Likewise, in looking down upon Lake Champlain from the campus of the University of Vermont in February, I marvel at that chilling, windswept expanse of ice-covered bleakness in tandem with a warm memory of gliding blithely across that rolling water at twilight on a balmy night with Nick and Nancy Muller in their sailboat. I marvel at climbing Camel's Hump on a warm June day and stepping gingerly not to injure the delicate Arctic vegetation which has established a southern outpost on this dramatic mountaintop. I marvel at lesser things, like Brian and Nancy Vachon's driveway in Montpelier: it is a graceful ascent in summer but a steep, slick, wheel-spinning coat of ice in the winter. One teeth-chattering evening I made it up but afterwards got stuck in a snowbank coming back down; the man who came to dinner stayed for breakfast.

I never cease to marvel that the sap which comes grudgingly from an ancient maple tree can be so sweet, that trout from the cold Willoughby River can be so tender, and that fiddlehead ferns growing along the upper Winooski River can be so tasty. A ham actor is usually a big eater, and the Vermont seasons accommodate my appetite for varied fare and nourishment.

A November snowfall may seem unjustly premature—winter is long enough without an early beginning—but, like Marguerite Wolf, I measure my ingratitude against the delight of learning what the wildlife has been doing because even a light dusting can preserve animal tracks as clues. An April snowstorm may seem unjustly excessive at the end of a hard winter, but maple producers who work in the sugarbush are thankful for it because it encourages the flow of sap. Long icicles on a spring day, as Governor George D. Aiken points out in the concluding essay of this book, can please a countryman because he knows it is a sure sign of maple sap running well. This book could have been titled differently with a slight change in wording: *Vermont: A Season for Every Person.*

Every person who contributed to the making of this book hopes you enjoy it. We hope you will experience your own discoveries about Vermont and share with us the constant marvel of living here. An "affinity with nature" goes hand-in-hand with an affinity for Vermont.

CHARLES T. MORRISSEY

Montpelier
January 1, 1980

VERMONT for Every Season

Winter's retreat is neither orderly nor measured each year. There is little precise or predictable in the annual passage from Vermont's longest acknowledged season to the shortest. Snow dawdles, skies threaten, puddles linger. And then suddenly it happens— signaled by the sun and confirmed in the freshness of the air. The new season has begun. The cycle itself begins again.

Downtown Woodstock, by William E. Hebden.

Still wintry white, Mt. Mansfield rises above spring's onset, by George C. Wilson; below, John Belding's photograph of red osiers is highlighted against a navy-blue sky; a Strafford farm amidst winter's melting snows, by R.J. Alzner.

Mist and melting snow cling to Barnet hillsides and a whitetail deer
listens expectantly, photographed by Richard W. Brown.
Warm weather causes an ice break-up in Richmond, by Paul O. Boisvert;
the yellow roadster is out of the barn early in the season,
photographed by Clyde H. Smith.

*Vanishing snows and budding trees signal the end of
winter in Peacham, by Clyde H. Smith.*

Days of Awakening

RONALD ROOD

It has been going on for days, even weeks. No telling, really, when it got started. Like a sound outside a window as you sleep, it gradually enters your consciousness until at last you are aware of it: the whisper of a wakening world.

It's a whisper as much sensed as heard. There are little changes in how things look and how they act. Sometimes how they smell, too.

In deepest winter the look of the land was largely black-gray-white, with bare twigs and branches and shadows etched against the snow. Now today there is, somehow, a difference. The lines are not as clearly drawn.

There's a suggestion of color as you look across the landscape. You cannot spot it in any one tree or shrub; it is too subtle for that. But the gray and black may be tinged with red or yellow or orange.

Silhouettes are altered. Elms and poplars and red maples seem to have larger buds than you remembered. New sap has entered their tissues, swelling each cell just a little.

Ponds and swamps and streams are different. Here and there the white mantle of snow has dropped in as the ice beneath it collapsed. These pits and pockets mark the course of a waterway and dot the surface of a lake.

Sometimes the weakening ice yields to the wind. It shifts a bit, opening a "lead" in the water. A ridge of ice appears at the lakeshore: a hint of the great thaw to come.

Nor is the snow the same. Earlier it was fluffy or powdery as layer added softly to layer. Now, long compressed from age and its own weight, the snow is coarser, more granular. Bits of bark and flecks of dust, absorbing the sun, melt their way into the snow until it becomes honeycombed.

Some of those specks are animated: spiders and caterpillars and craneflies, and snowfleas or springtails. Their dark-colored bodies soak up warmth as they explore the boulders and caverns of their ice-crystal world.

The bark on a tree is sheltering an entire insect zoo. It has been biding its time. Now the bark is a launching pad for cluster flies, little brown moths, ladybird beetles and gnats. They crawl from beneath their shelter, out into the chilly air. You learn of them as the birds desert your feeder for the tree bark buffet.

Each day, the sun stays about two minutes longer. Then you begin to hear distant calls, like the barking of dogs, or the shreds of a muffled conversation, and then you realize what it is. There is the welcome flock; the geese so incredibly high that individual members can barely be distinguished. Their cries are returned by birds in the forests and fields. All winter the smaller ones have followed the same routine, day after day. Now they, too, are changing.

The chickadee has a new urge. No longer will a chatty recitation of its name suffice. It must sing a different song: two high whistles, the second slightly lower than the first. The clear double-note lasts for only a second, and it certifies the creature's potential as a parent—even though nesting season is yet months away.

Other birds respond to the awakening. Nuthatches have visited the feeder all winter, male indistinguishable from female. Now, the difference between them becomes apparent. The male spreads his wings at the approach of a female, and she, in turn, may flutter and beg. Obligingly, the male selects a sunflower seed and presents it to her.

Out comes a woodpecker from his tree to select a spot that resounds just right, and he hammers it rapidly in a loud tattoo. The noise echoes through the woods—a promise that, when mating season comes, he's there. And he's available.

The restlessness extends to cities and suburbs. Pigeons leave village street and city park for an hour or two to explore possible homes beneath bridges, on fire escapes and along window ledges. Starlings still help themselves at your feeder, but they also inspect that hole up under the eaves.

A red fox trots through the night. Now and again it utters a throaty bark—a challenge or an invitation, depending on the sex of the intended listener. Sometimes, in its exuberance, the fox yelps and yaps its way into a farmyard. Sometimes it strays into the suburbs, setting off an uproar among the neighborhood dogs.

There may be another cause of commotion, too. Your stately garbage can suddenly takes a turn for the worse. Now, with clever hands busy and chunky body straining, the raccoon decapitates the trash barrel—or uproots it entirely.

Skunks—opportunists that they are—seem to regard anything as fair game: a drowsy grub, a beetle, or the remains of a sandwich. Skunks are placid creatures, but almost nightly you can expect a whiff of perfume from some putterer.

Then there's the fragrance of the wood-kitty's namesake, the skunk cabbage. Buried a foot or so in the icy mud of a swamp or streamside, it activates a chemical laboratory in its tissues, releasing heat and energy. The heat warms the ground, and the plant melts its way to the surface. There the skunk cabbage stands in the late-winter snow. Its pointed hood shelters a fetid-smelling flower which looks like a tiny ear of corn, and it pours out an aroma like a refrigerator gone bad. Those early rising flies and beetles crawl over pollen and pistil in their search for the decaying meat—and next year's skunk cabbages are on the way.

Other plants emerge from the softening earth. A crocus blossoms in the snow. The snow recedes from lawn and garden and border, and you see the points of tulip and narcissus and daffodil. They look as if they've been there all winter. Yet you know there was not a sign of them last fall.

You and I are also aware of the summons. We need no calendar to tell of the approaching season. Nor do we require seed catalogues, end-of-winter sales, or mud puddles inviting youngsters to slosh and splash. Something indefinable prompts us to get out the golf clubs, the fishing rod or tennis racket for a fond appraisal. We exhume last year's summer clothing to see if we can make it do for another season.

The convertible appears on the streets. So do motorcycles, dodging the icy spots and vaulting over frost heaves. Baseballs, bats and gloves come out of hibernation. Sunbathers materialize in lawnchairs or on porch roofs. In their annual ritual they gain a chill and a burn at the same time.

The pace quickens. Snow crystals dissolve into meltwater. The water drips from fallen twig and grassy hummock. It trickles over moss and rocks, and gathers into rivulets. These join to form temporary brooks, and together they hurry to some larger stream.

The ice of creek and river yields to the flood. It loses its grip on shoreline and boulders—and even on itself, as large cracks appear over its surface. It breaks into great chunks. Slicing over each other, hurtling along at a desperate pace, the chunks roar downstream. They burst over the banks and out into the fields.

The juggernaut sweeps along, half water, half ice. It scars the trunks of large streamside trees and rides up over smaller ones. Then, in the space of a quarter hour, it subsides. The ice has gone out. The stream has roused itself.

As the snow retreats, the fields are already a hopeful green. A pussy willow blooms along the roadside. The early dandelion is joined by dozens more; soon there will be thousands. The alder lets down a host of golden catkins. Everywhere, things are greener. Buds are bigger—or they burst entirely.

Here is a harbinger robin; there a grackle or redwing. Each, as it flies northward, calls to tree and rock and mountain. And, from skunk and snowflea, crow and crocus, sunbather warming under a blue sky and frog chortling in the icy water, comes the answer:

"All right—all right! We were awake long ago!"

Now there are just short weeks for a whole countryside of plants and animals to lay the foundation for coming generations. They've got their work cut out for them this time of year. Sometimes there are only days.

The early woodland flowers, for instance, need the rich and scented humus, the coolness and moisture of the forest floor—and yet they need the sun. When the leaves appear on the trees and the green canopy closes overhead, the sunshine will be blotted out. Those plants have to walk a tightrope in that fleeting time between the warming of the soil and the waning of the sun.

It's no accident that bloodroot and spring beauty, trillium and dogtooth violet bloom today while the trees are scarcely bursting their buds. They've got to; tomorrow will be too late.

Trees, shrubs and other plants do their seeking through pioneers sent out. Pine and poplar and alder, among others, strew their billions of pollen grains on the breeze. The pollen puffs away with every zephyr, and launches golden clouds toward the slim possibility that a few particles will find the waiting pistils of others of their kind.

Most of the grains drift fruitlessly. When the air is stilled and their luck runs out, the record of their failure is a filmy yellow layer on the circling eddies of ponds and brooks.

Dandelion parachutes, as many as a hundred from each whitened head, rise up and away, gleaming above your head. Marsh marigold flowers wither into seed pods that drop to the waters that gave them birth. They drift along: little brown boats, silent.

Even the seeds of last year may just now be getting their start. They dropped in the fall but may have done little more than lie on the chilly earth. Now they sink into their cradle.

There is no time to waste in the farmer's fields, either. Crop plants, many of them, are native to warmer climes than ours. Squashes and pumpkins and beans come from the semi-tropics, as do potato, corn, and tomato. To them a single freeze is deadly and final while the same icy chill may give our more hardy native plants no more than a minor setback.

The sun is warm on the farmer's back as rows are made by the heavy work of plowing. It is good to stretch those muscles, to dig hard and deep, to know the satisfaction of sweaty labor. The smell of that new-turned soil brings a sense of accomplishment.

The same sense continues to pervade all of our lives. June becomes the month of weddings, and the Vermont hills provide a living cathedral.

On the farm, the shepherd has carefully counted the lambs as they appeared in the springing flock. Many of them were born while it was yet cold and wintry. Most of them made it, but here's one that seems to be having trouble. Into the house it goes— there to be cuddled and wheedled.

Wobbly calves, gangling colts, pink pigs that scamper on clicking hoofs, all add their promise to that of downy chicks and speckled poults and powderpuff ducklings. Birds of a hundred species pluck and weave and hammer and sing and fight. Gnats playing above a quiet pond, bass and perch and frogs and toads in its shallows—all agree: this is the time to sow. We ourselves agree as we scratch into the earth with hoe and plow. Not tomorrow or the next day, but now.

William Hebden's East Corinth scene awaits spring's greening.

A country road winds around a Northeast Kingdom farm, photographed by Richard W. Brown; in Tunbridge, sheep graze contentedly on the season's first grass, by Hanson Carroll.

On early Spring days, when the ground is still too wet
for a tractor, a man and his team have an excuse to
work together and to harden winter-softened muscles.
There is an art to plowing and a rhythm and functional
beauty to the mutual effort. Furrow upon furrow,
the earth peels back from the blade, forming a patch of
brown corduroy without a fleck of green showing.

Horse teams photographed by Richard W. Brown.

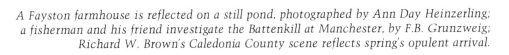

*A Fayston farmhouse is reflected on a still pond, photographed by Ann Day Heinzerling;
a fisherman and his friend investigate the Battenkill at Manchester, by F.B. Grunzweig;
Richard W. Brown's Caledonia County scene reflects spring's opulent arrival.*

Marsh marigolds surround an ancient split rail fence, by Lud Munchmeyer; Dutchman's breeches, photographed by Ottar Indridason.

Richard W. Brown's warbler welcomes
spring; Stephen T. Whitney's bloodroot
blooms in Spencer Hollow and Ottar
Indridason's trout lily flourishes in Gifford
Woods. Marjorie Ryerson's dandelion
picker near Randolph is her son.

Apple trees burst into fragrant lace, photographed in North Hartland (left) by John Harris, and in Hartford (above) by R.J. Alzner who appears in his own tranquil scene.

Mist covered Mt. Equinox overlooks a newly plowed field, photographed by Lud Munchmeyer; below, Paul O. Boisvert photographed this Brownsville farmer sowing his ample garden; right, spring planting begins in South Strafford, by Hanson Carroll.

Days to Savor

ANNE O'LEARY

Summer is upon us once again. Memorial Day marks an influx of visitors which will continue summer-long until the last remaining families head back to the cities on Labor Day. Villages all over Vermont burst with new faces, and familiar ones which have been absent since the last time the June breezes heralded Vermont's time to savor. The rich bounty of delightful days will pass more rapidly than we ever realize, but we are compensated by a myriad of fairs and strawberry festivals, parades and picnics that no other season rivals. Vermont towns in the summer swell like flowers in bloom.

Even the daily chores seem lighter in summer. The day lasts so long there's time to work hard and play hard and just laze around, too. School is out; the birthings of spring are done with. There's no wood to be cut or stacked or split just yet. And it's not quite time to begin the labor of harvesting and canning and freezing. There's no snow to be shoveled, no fires to be stoked. Only the mowing, gardening, and painting yet another side of the big red barn require our attention. And these are chores to be shared with family and friends. There's a sense of leisure everywhere. Yes, the chores must be done, but summer doesn't insist, summer doesn't threaten like winter does. From break of day till evening's advent and beyond, Vermonters celebrate each sweet, warm moment in a summer day.

Blue chicory blossoms and pea vetch, daisies and clover color the fields and cluster along stone walls. The grape vines tumble over the trellis, and perfume the air. Even the house plants—voluptuous bursts of geraniums, scarlet and hot pink, cool spiderplants, ferns and ivy, outside at last—deck the porches, hanging from baskets or balancing on old wicker stands.

Colorful posters hang on the thumbtack-speckled clapboard of the general store advertising a play at the town hall, a raffle, free kittens and mongrel dogs. High schoolers, available to mow the lawn, weed the garden, babysit or do odd jobs, tack index cards hand-printed with name, phone and hourly wages on the bulletin board. A small, neatly typed notice for the auction of an entire farm mars the carefree summer mood. By the weekend antique dealers and tourists, farmers and townspeople, hoping to salvage something useful from the demise of another working farm, will rummage through the years of memories and hard work left behind by a family that couldn't withstand the battle of spiraling costs and low return.

Folding metal chairs arranged in straggling rows will stretch across the yard and from under the shade of the back porch the auctioneer will hawk his goods. Rush-bottomed chairs and wash stands, maple-framed mirrors and portraits of stiff-backed ancestors, tools and farm implements will be paraded before the crowd until the old house stands barren. But newcomers in search of a summer house, perhaps, or an old homestead in the country will snap up these goods and paint them, fix them, and enjoy them anew.

Through the thick cover of maples overhead, patches of sunlight stream in dusty motes onto the sidewalk where village neighbors stop to chat. The leaves cast a dense green tint on the still hot air and heat waves rise shimmering from the pavement in the relentless midday sun. "We sure could use some rain," someone says in the thick late-afternoon air. But dark clouds edge over the horizon, rumbling as they draw nearer. The first drops of rain splat onto the dirt roads, raising puffs of dust. Faster and faster they fall until the surface of the road is pocked with dark, wet spots, and then the clouds open, drenching the fields and forests. Children beg to be allowed to run and dance in the heavy rain. Annoyed mothers rush to the clothes line where the day's laundry already hangs limp. The heat spell has at last been broken and the freshly washed evening air will make sleeping easier at last.

Sunlight whitens the bedroom ceiling by 5:30 a.m. It's too early, and I roll over and try to steal a few more minutes of sleep. A fly dives and circles overhead, bumping against the screens, and robins and thrushes screech and haggle from tree to tree, announcing the arrival of sky-blue eggs in one nest, or the dangers of the farmhouse cat. I pull the thin muslin sheet over my head, burrow my face in the pillow for a minute and suddenly sit up, awake. Morning has begun—a good two hours before I'd ever get up on a wintry morn.

But instead of bundling into layers of woolen clothes, hopping from foot to foot on the frigid floor boards, hoping someone else has the fire already

A Cambridge farm is cradled among lush, new summer growth, by Norman MacIver.

blazing, I quickly slip into a sheer cotton shirt and pull on blue jeans faded with age. Shoeless, hair brushed back, I patter barefoot down the wooden stair treads, through the kitchen, still quiet, and out onto the porch, slamming the screen door behind me.

The air is still cool; the sun is more bright than hot at this hour. I skim the two stone slab steps and feel the chill of the cold, wet grass, ankle-deep, thick and green, as I cross the yard towards the dusty path that leads to the lake. Gravelly stones hurt my feet, still soft with sleep, and shivering I wrap my arms around myself, clutching my shoulders for warmth. The horses lift their heads from grazing to watch as I pass their meadow still pale with morning dew.

As I near the pond I slow to a tiptoe gait and cautiously tread around the last, obscuring copse of birch. Mist rolls off the slate-gray water. There's not a sound: the frogs have anticipated my arrival and soundlessly listen for footsteps. For a tense, still moment only the cry of a redwing blackbird slivers the air.

Quietly I approach the pond, straining hopefully to see and hear if anything is lurking in the tangle of cattails at the pond's edge. Suddenly a beaver slides into the water with a mighty plop and descends to swimming depths. A doe leaps from the grass into the white pine stand on the opposite bank, and again all is still. These are the joys of being the first one up on a Vermont summer morning.

Quickly, I slip off my jeans and shirt. The cool air swirls around my naked skin and for a second I feel goosebumps everywhere. With a running start I plunge into the lake. The tepid water lulls my taut, chill-braced skin as I strike out with tireless strokes, back and forth. One lap, two laps. Enough. Without drying I pull on my clothes. They snag against my damp, resisting skin and I run as fast as I can back to the house.

I smell coffee from across the yard. Crossing the porch I bang the screen door behind me again and jubilantly announce to the sleepier members of the family gathered around the kitchen table, "I just saw a big beaver and a doe at the lake!"

Eagerly and hungrily I carry a plate of muffins and a dish of fresh, sweet butter out onto the porch. A big glass bowl of strawberries, fresh from the garden patch, a jug of heavy cream and a wedge of honeycomb glinting golden are already on the bench outside. Steaming mugs of freshly ground coffee are carried out last and the whole family, visiting friends, Cousin Kate and Uncle Charles, even the cat, join us for a Vermont summer break-fast alfresco. The sun is getting hotter, but everyone lingers, biting into one more ripe, scarlet berry dripping with beads of honey, making plans for the day.

Gradually the drone of a tractor rises from the northwest corner of the meadow. Time to get to work: our neighbor has the tractor, but we have to rake the hay for his goats by hand. A simple barter: he gets the hay which is too fine for horses, and we get the meadow mowed. And with so many hands the work will be over by noon and then there will still be enough to do to fill a week of days.

By 11:00 a.m. the sun is searingly hot, almost overhead. The hay is mounded in neat cones scattered evenly across the meadow and our muscles ache from the work and heat. The scent of the freshly mowed grass is so lush it almost stifles us. We are lulled, and only feel sad that the daisies and purple asters, fiery orange hawk weed and Queen Anne's lace fell before the mower's blade as well. A nest of field mice has been devastated by the tractor's weight, and the discovery of the quills and skull of a porcupine, possibly frozen or starved by winter's bitter cold, reminds us that summer is, indeed, nature's brief reprieve.

We turn toward the farmhouse, rakes bouncing on our sunburned shoulders, the children running ahead. Someone proposes a cooling splash in the lake and another suggests we raid the garden for a lunch of tender salad greens, radishes, raw fresh peas and chives. We all concur and flinging our rakes against the garden fence, dash toward the pond. Everyone joins in dunking, but the fun is short-lived since we are hungry from our morning's work.

We divide the labor of lunch: some of us pick vegetables, some of us prepare them. The children shell the peas, giggling and sneaking whole podfuls into their mouths. Uncle Charles worries us with his visions of woodchucks in the tomato patch and raccoons in the corn.

We'll have to stake the "Have-a Hearts," he says, and wails of distress greet his intention. Six-year-old Kate admonishes him, "Raccoons have families too, Uncle Charles. You can't break up a family because of corn!"

Abruptly the toot of a car horn halts our discord. Peering from the kitchen light into the cool darkness of the house we see our summer neighbors, up for a week from the city, striding into the front hall. With immense pleasure we exchange hugs and greetings, invite them to stay for lunch and catch up on the news of the past nine months. But they are too eager to share in Vermont's summer life to dwell on what the city has offered them. They are bursting with plans for the next five days and we decide to join them when we can.

We picnic in the yard again, juggling bowls of salad and glasses of minted ice tea on the arms of wicker rocking chairs. The children gobble their lunches and gallop off to catch the horses for an afternoon of exploration. The woods are checkered with old, abandoned roads and trails and the nimble little Morgan mares, Vermont's equine pride, pick their ways agilely over stone walls and through chest-high brush. The bay filly, newly weaned, squeals from the paddock in anguished distress as her dam trots merrily down the road, her bare-backed young rider swaying with each pert step. We are reminded of our own younger years in the Green Mountains as we watch them wind their way out of sight down the dusty lane.

By dusk the day's work is done: the meadow is mowed and raked, the garden weeded. A trap lies in wait to cage a thieving woodchuck or coon. At our neighbor's suggestion we have shared in the delicious task of picking quarts and quarts of firm blueberries and pints of fragrant jam now cool on the pantry shelf. The weaning foal has had her halter lesson and the children are sorting wildflowers and mushrooms they have gathered on their ride. They make plans to hunt frogs tomorrow.

But tonight we will attend a performance of a summer music festival as we do at least once each summer. Every July and August throughout the state, music festivals—classical, rock and folk—lure appreciative listeners to grassy amphitheaters. We bundle in sweaters and wiggle wool-stockinged feet into summer sandals to prevent the chill night air from dampening our high spirits. Blankets are spread on the sloping lawns and as the strains of Mozart and Haydn, or Dylan and Joplin, resound from the woods and hillsides, we lie back, children nestled against parents, and couples side by side, to listen to the music soar across the dense black night. The solemn simple beauty of such a summer night lingers for years thereafter; each time we step outside to glimpse a harvest moon, or catch our final breath of frigid winter air under the starry sky, we recall the majesty of each season in Vermont and wonder how we can be so blessed with so much beauty.

The corn will soon be ready—if the coons decide to share—and the blackberries are almost ripe. The owls are hooting nightly now, their tragic calls menacing the quiet slumber of rodents everywhere, and the raucous, gaudy storms of August evenings extinguish our electrified lifestyles with annoying regularity.

Another cousin is coming to visit and more neighbors will soon be here. The flea market is at its height and there will be plenty of memorabilia to pick through there. Long tables hem the Common each Saturday morning and homemade pastries, hand-knit caps and mittens for winter, pots of herbs, garden vegetables, old books and loads of attic junk are piled high. The hospital fair with its fine selection of patchwork quilts is on Sunday, and soon the fire department will be barbecuing its annual chicken dinner on the Common.

Summer is in full bloom.

Farmscape in East Randolph, by R.J. Alzner.

A flock of sheep graze in a Northeast Kingdom meadow, by Richard W. Brown; a woolly sheep and its shepherds are photographed by Hanson Carroll in Tunbridge; in Orwell, cheviot lambs check out photographer Lud Munchmeyer.

Lush green hills and fertile fields surround
the Howe farm in Tunbridge, VDA; a farmer sharpens
a cutter for haying, photographed by
John A. Lynch; the Cilley Bridge at Tunbridge
frames this view photographed by Cecile Briggs.

And, finally, along comes summer—sure and warm and unmistakable. It's a busy time, a time to be grasped and used and savored.

Fresh strawberries and a
little girl's giggle are sights
and sounds of summer in
Hartland, by Ava Emerson;
camps on Woodbury Pond provide
a setting for relaxation and
solitude, by Norman MacIver;
joggers run alongside shimmering
Lake Champlain in Grand Isle,
photographed by Richard Howard.

43

Summer Celebrations include the chicken barbecue at Chelsea
Old Home Day, photographed by Suzanne Opton; two friends enjoying
a moment of leisure in Bethel, by Ava Emerson; at the Warren
Fourth of July, Peter Miller's camera recorded the two-man saw
cutting contest; opposite, Sam Ogden leads the traditional
Landgrove July 4th party, photographed by Ellen Foscue Johnson.

*Attracted by the conviviality, the kaleidoscope
of color, the cacophony of sound,
everyone is drawn to a summer's celebration.*

The hard work and long hours of haying fill the extended
days of summer; above, a moment of relaxation in Peacham and,
top right, haying at the Robb Farm in Brattleboro,
photographed by Richard Howard; below, Richard W. Brown
records a day's labors in the Northeast Kingdom.

*Summer campers enjoy sailboat ride on
Lake Fairlee, by Margaretta Mitchell.*

The spectacular view for these Long Trail hikers is worth the climb, photograph by Hanson Carroll.

A pipe-smoking observer contemplates the merchandise and the auctioneer acknowledges a bid for the old windup phonograph, photographs by Clyde H. Smith. Opposite, family estate auction in Morrisville, by Stuart E. Bertland.

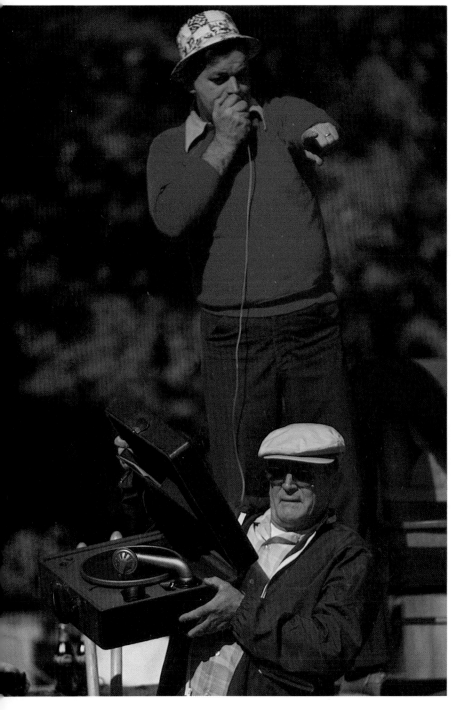

Summer is auction time. For the serious Vermont-style shopper there is no substitute. Inveterate auctiongoers, dealers, summer visitors and neighbors arrive looking for the ultimate bargain, intriguing items or a particular functional piece. And some people come to just plain observe.

The sharp blues and greens at summer's height
are recorded by Richard W. Brown in his
photograph of Mt. Mansfield; a jersey near
a stream in Woodstock, photographed by
Zelda Glasser; Jane Meiklejohn's photograph of
Worcester reflects the serenity of a small town.

A brook rushes, slides and gurgles over
rock, carving out smooth forms and
sharp crevices, sculptured by the water
and ice of a thousand summers and
winters. Cutting through the woods,
surrounded by overhanging trees, a brook
secludes and mesmerizes. And suddenly,
the stream spills into a huge rock
hole. Like a knot in a tree, the pool
causes a bulge in the curving line
of the brook's direction. The water is
still here, and clear.

*Camouflaged by tree-lined rock walls, these swimming holes
provide a cool relief, photographed by Peter Miller.*

*Wilmington's Main Street, photographed by Jane Cooper;
a quiet moment in Pawlet, by Clyde H. Smith;
in Randolph, a cool and shaded summer porch, by Marjorie Ryerson.*

The fine red barn in Dummerston was photographed by Cecile Briggs; clouds float over the Champlain Valley with the Adirondacks in the background, by John F. Smith; on a country road near Peacham, Richard W. Brown photographed a boy herding the cows home.

A flock of sheep in the rosy glow of sunset near the Leo Hutchinson Farm in East Corinth, by Hans Wendler; an evening's concert at the Webb Estate in Shelburne, photographed by Clyde H. Smith; in William Hebden's photograph, darkness descends on a farm in East Corinth.

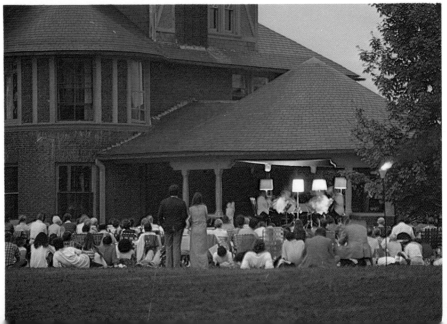

The end of a summer day arrives softly, almost shyly; a gentle pastel sunset yields to a midnight-blue sky, the day's labors end and the invulnerable lamplights of home glow warmly.

Harvest time approaches in Richard W. Brown's photograph of a Northeast Kingdom farm; Richard Howard photographs farmers' markets in Montpelier (left), Randolph (above) and Newport (right).

Shucking corn at the Harold Harrington Farm in North Pomfret, by Hanson Carroll.

Days to Harvest

DONNA FITCH

Summer ends when lush and leisurely days slip deceptively into a different time span and we waken one morning and find ourselves asking, "Now, *where* did the summer go?"

There's no longer time to sit on the front porch and stare the simmering heat waves down as they waft across the field. Abruptly, time is short and we're bound to say, "There's just not enough hours in the day."

Suddenly, it's harvest time.

It's hard to believe the amount of work to be done before the cool nights of fall turn into the freezing nights of winter. It's equally hard to believe that in three, maybe four, months we will waken to the first smattering of snow, that a shovel will replace the hoe that stands ready by the back door.

You'd think we would come to expect these changes. But, no, each year the end of summer unexpectedly arrives and we're caught as unaware as the year before. Quickly, we make lists and jot down duties we know we'll never finish before wintry drafts ooze under doors and around windows. "Shuck corn and freeze; bring in squash; clear cobwebs from root cellar; buy new chainsaw blade; sharpen axe; check chimneys; finish pickling cukes." One list inevitably leading to another.

Yes, summer ends when we least expect it. The land is verdant, roadsides are overgrown, the tall, jungle-like grasses reach out to grab us as we drive by. Voluptuous trees form cathedral-like arches above the roadways, leaving a protected passageway which frames the dirt road in emerald green. Standing within this tree-lined tunnel we're protected from the summer sun and strain to see the sky peeking through the tightly woven leaves.

Window boxes drip flowers flaunting their opulent and full-colored petals. Houses stand tall and straight as if awaiting an inspection. Lawns are smooth and neatly trimmed; any evidence of winter's strain or a spring storm's damage has long since faded away.

And when we're feeling that the season is surely at its height, our summer neighbor comes to say goodbye. Suddenly, we're made aware of the one red maple among the green, of the shortened days and browning weeds. The zucchini have passed their zenith; the corn is more than ripe.

Where have we been that summer's end has snuck up on us, made us turn full circle and is now staring us cold in the face? Summer's clever, she is. She gives us one last gaudy exhibition. One last splashy show before her curtain call. We applaud for more, we *hope* for more. But no encore by summer. No, once she's gone, she's gone. Maybe a bit of Indian Summer will happen to release us gradually into autumn, to let us down slowly from hot, muggy days to the clear, warm days of fall. But it's certainly not the same intensity that we have come to take for granted.

We take summer's disappearance much more seriously than she. She flashes off and into autumn colors before we know what's happened. There will be many seasons before we see her again. She seems to enjoy her trickery, slipping off when we've just become accustomed to her sunny atmosphere, her balmy disposition.

Summer's leave-taking is almost searing. There's a lingering sadness, a feeling of culmination. We never feel this way in May, and even autumn's splendid ornamentation cannot completely alleviate our feelings of something lost. Summer leaves us with lots to do and we have little time to mourn her disappearance. Once again we're reminded: it's harvest time.

Time to get in the rowen. Time to squeeze one last bale into the haymow. Time to take a peek at the *Farmer's Almanac*, or check a caterpillar's rings or the toughness of a squash's skin, to estimate winter's severity. If the signs point to a mild winter, we don't take it as a guarantee. Even a mild winter means snow and wind and freezing temperatures. That's inevitable. What we store away in our silos and haymows, in our cellars and freezers, is what we have to depend on to feed our animals and ourselves through the upcoming winter months, "mild" or not.

So we give the hayfields one last going over. The fox, which followed us from field to field this summer waiting for the short-cropped grass to expose the field mouse's home, is no longer scrutinizing us from the woodside shadows. This summer he seemed to think his appearance was essential to the haying process, but now he's too busy preparing his lair to worry about a few field mice and our last mowing. We might see him again, however, before next summer. We're apt to catch a glimpse of him, or at least his tracks, when we cross-country ski through the deeper, denser woods this winter.

No longer subjugated to the fox's game of hide and seek, the mice can rest easy now and prepare their evacuation to warmer places—barns and houses being the most comfortable winter accommodations. Scuttling through the walls, they're apt to wake us on a winter's night, causing us to huddle deeper under the covers, and reminding us of the sweet, musty smell of new-mown hay, of the fox and her young by the field edge and of the warmth of the summer sun on our backs.

The deer stay with us through the harvest. As if helping with the last haying, they graze the fields for their evening meal (and passersby are given hardly a glance). Though their dinner isn't as sumptuous as it was when they stood belly deep in the tall, sweet grass, they realize time is short before the hunters' guns and winter's ice and snow converge upon their territory.

We understand how the deer feel. Winter's encroachment invades our summer indolence. We've been caught languishing and now there's work to do.

Expectation of the first frost hurries us along. The generosity of our garden amazes us as we view the culmination of her yield. Canning and freezing reaches its peak. On the stove canners bubble, pressure cookers steam. Jars are sterilized and waiting open-mouthed to be filled with sweet or sour pickles, relish or cardinal-red tomatoes. Though we're always ready to try a new recipe, usually after sampling a neighbor's green tomato relish ("Now, what is that herb I taste?") or watermelon pickles, we tend to stand by our grandmothers' and greatgrandmothers' methods. We follow the faded directions penned down decades ago on a slip of paper, the writing more distinct where following generations have written their additions and suggestions and where we'll add our comments, too.

We swap talk and recipes with our neighbors, discuss our garden's bounty, analyze her downfalls.

"My winter squash didn't do too well this year. I've only got a bushel. And I'm worried the frost will catch the tomatoes before they're fully ripe."

"It's the same with me. But the zucchini and summer squash certainly made up for the winter squash."

"The zucchini always do well."

The zucchini are turning into blimps and we've exhausted every recipe. There was a touch of frost last night and we've developed culinary methods to deal with the onslaught of green tomatoes. We've more than enough piccalilli to last us through the winter and to give away to friends.

For a special treat we've made brandied peaches. Their sweet and fruity taste will be especially welcome a few months from now. We've frozen peas, beans, beets and corn. And fruit too: strawberries, blueberries, raspberries, blackberries. We open the freezer door and take joy at the sight of colorful rows of hard work, a season's harvest.

We're picking cauliflower and broccoli long after the first frost. We steam it, casserole it, sauce it, soup it until we're so sick of it we can't imagine looking forward to its homegrown taste next year. We almost forget that we'll be eyeing the grocery store prices in mid-January with a self-satisfied glance that *we* don't have to pay those prices. We've got a freezer full.

Now we spend our days deepening the path from the kitchen to the garden. Many hours are spent inside but it doesn't feel that way. Our vegetables remind us of the days outside preparing and sowing our garden, of the time spent weeding. And through the screen door we hear the corn chopper droning down the rows of cows' corn.

The sound of a corn chopper is a sure sign that it's time to reap. The hay is in and now it's the corn's turn to fill plump silos. It's time for a community corn roast, for that delicious taste of sweet corn roasted in its husk in the coals of a wood fire. It's the best moment for a respite from the feeling that, as Robert Frost wrote, "I am overtired of the great harvest I myself desired."

Churches and community organizations take advantage of a garden's excess, and a chance to make a little money for a roof repair or choir robes, by hosting boiled dinners or maybe even offering red flannel hash or baked beans and brown bread. One thing you know you can expect is a variety of pies: apple, pumpkin, mincemeat.

The sounds of this period of the year are unique. A soothing quiet pervades. The children are back in school. We hear the school bus rumble by twice a day. The fields have been plowed under and lie fallow, almost desolate and very empty, waiting to shiver with the first frosts and then freeze and be blanketed by snow. Working, head down, concentrating on some important task, we suddenly hear a honking and no task is so important that we can't leave it to look up at the V of the Canada geese flying south.

The smell of autumn is with us, lingering in our nostrils even when we're not outside: drying grasses, leaves crushed beneath our feet, freshly cut wood and now and again the smell of wood smoke, the first warming fires of this cooler season. The smell of ripe apples, and the plops of their falling to the ground, is the cue to bring out the cider press. The incomparable taste of fresh apple cider is surely a sign that the apple tree is attempting to compete with the maple and that first taste of maple syrup in the spring.

We gather drops from the orchard and shake the apple trees to get any McIntosh that have not been eaten, put into pies, apple pan dowdy or frozen. The Macs now meet their fate in the grinder box of the cider press along with the wild apples we've gathered on forays to the back woods, or on some knoll in an overgrown pasture.

Bunched together and hanging upside down to dry, our garden herbs will lend a fresh aroma in the months to come when our winterized house is closed up tight. From down by the brook we've picked mint for tea and the plants' tiny, purple flowers add a touch of color to the fading greenness of the herbs.

The first frost has hit. We've rescued the last remnants of our garden and covered what flowers we could—a few still linger. Talk turns to wood and winter things. How many cords did we burn last year? How many cords have we cut so far and how much yet to go? One more trip to that stand of beech just to make sure. We eye our neighbors' wood piles. Each pile stands unique as if a reflection of the stacker. One pile is precisely stacked, neat, erect. Another, almost tumbling, and will, we think, with six inches of snow or more.

The days have shortened. It's dark by 7 p.m. And while the days are still warm, it's sweater weather and the evenings are cool. We're building fires at night now, to edge the cold back for a time at least. The summer people have all left. We're battling cluster flies and wasps; they're creeping in from the cold.

And though there's plenty to do—fasten down the shutters, put on storm windows, insulate the cellar door and windows—a period of waiting sets in. We stop a moment in our work to peruse all that we've accomplished, all that we have reaped. This is a chance to stop, reflect and look around. We even have the time, or take the time, to become a bit philosophical.

It is a necessary time to prepare ourselves, our minds, to gather our thoughts before the solitariness of winter, to store away in our memory the pleasures of our summer activities, of gatherings with family and friends. We look back at the months we've come through. We check our progress. We hesitate. We almost want to stop the flow of the seasons, to remain suspended for a while.

These feelings are more vivid at harvest time than at any other. It's a time of realization and, though it happens every year, once again it's like a new discovery. We feel fulfilled; it's the one time when we would never question our reason for being. There's a direct connection between our labors and our survival. We reappreciate the importance of our land, of our dependence on nature, of this very special way of life we have in Vermont.

It's the feeling of being connected with the land, with our neighbors, with our family, with Vermont. It's a sensation we might call "being one with nature," or with God.

It's the awareness of our continuity with the seasons. The importance, and yet the simplicity, of our lives. The poignant feeling of beginnings and endings, and how one flows to and through another. We almost catch a glimpse of the "why" of things.

And when these feelings become so intense we think we can't possibly hold them inside us any longer, we put a coat around our shoulders and slip outside some evening and watch the harvest moon rise big and round and orange.

We've prepared ourselves for winter, arranged our thoughts and drawn conclusions. Our house is tightly bundled. The woodpile's stacked high. Jars of pickles, relishes, tomatoes and chutney line the cellar shelves. Tucked away in dark root cellars, the winter squash and potatoes are hibernating. The freezer's full, the haymow and silo too. The crops are in. Finally, we have brought the harvest home.

A hint of color signals the start of autumn, photographed at the floating bridge in Brookfield, by Marjorie Ryerson.

Opposite page, harvesting begins in earnest as attested to by David Cain's Clarendon Flats garden photograph (left), Richard Howard's photograph taken at the Morrisville Farmers' Market (right) and a community garden in Shelburne, photographed by Peter Coleman (bottom). Business is steady at the Norwich Farmers' Market (above) and in Montpelier (lower right), photographed by Richard Howard; harvesting potatoes in Albany, by Stephen T. Whitney (above right).

Summer's end is marked by children returning to school, photographed
by Richard Howard at the Robb Farm in Brattleboro; and shadows lengthen
upon the subdued colors of a cooler earth in West Haven, by Clyde H. Smith.

A misty morning in East Montpelier,
by Clyde H. Smith; the last remnants
of the garden are protected
from the first frosts as photographed
by Marjorie Ryerson in Randolph
Center; the sun-shrouded hills
around Barnet rise above the morning
fog, by Richard W. Brown.

On misty mornings, the gentle time of day, all of nature's
intricacies stand revealed by wafted dew. Beneath dawn's gray
cloak, whispy vapor floats skyward from little ponds and
quiet streams. Each blade of grass shimmers with
morning magic; rolling hills glitter in golden light.
And the mists occur all autumn long, rolling in cool air over
warm earth and marking the progress of a closing year.

*Marching band at the Tunbridge Fair,
by Richard Howard; horse pulling at the
Danville Fair, by Richard W. Brown.*

*Judging cows and doughnuts at the
Tunbridge Fair, by Richard Howard; a young
Danville Fair goer, by Richard W. Brown.*

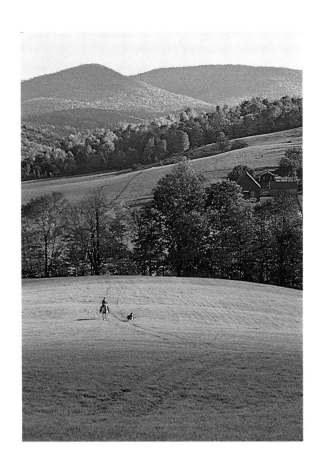

*An early mirror of autumn is captured by Geoffrey C. Clifford's
horseback rider in West Windsor; Richard W. Brown's Northeast
Kingdom landscape, and Hans Wendler's Silver Lake near Barnard.*

In the Northeast Kingdom, burnt reds and greenish-yellow creep down a hillside until they burst forth in a full-color display, a hint of the brilliance to come; a woman and her cat return from the garden, photographs by Richard W. Brown.

Vapor from the breath of cows rises in the chilly morning air
as photographed by Geoffrey C. Clifford in West Windsor; mist rises
in the aerial view of Barnet by Richard W. Brown.

82

Annemarie Busch photographed this Pomfret farmer doing his chores against
the backdrop of a graying hillside; in Randolph Center, a farmer
directs a cow down a leaf-strewn lane, photographed by Joseph A. DiChello, Jr.

Woodpiles and woodchoppers give evidence of another change in season, as recorded by John Belding in East Orange (top left) and in Barre (bottom left); colorful foliage begins to exceed the green in George A. Robinson's Jericho photograph below.

METHODIST PARKING

Luminous maples line a leaf-covered drive near Grafton, by R.J. Alzner.

Days of Splendor

REEVE BROWN

Each year it takes us by surprise. Each year we are caught unprepared and disbelieving until faced with the full-blown, indisputable spectacle of Vermont foliage. We had completely forgotten it was quite *this* lovely. I am not even sure that the human mind can remember so much beauty for as long as an entire year. A little of it slips away each month until, by early September, we have diminished the memory of fall to some mere and seasonal prettiness over which we can quibble and reminisce with neighbors.

"Looks dry. I guess the foliage won't be too good this year," someone tells me every autumn.

"Probably not as good as last year," I offer. "But then no year is."

"Too much rain," a different authority insists. "You won't see the color for a while yet."

But it is early. The season has not had time to ripen. The last of the hay has just been cut, the apples have not yet been brought to full flavor by frost, and the trees are looking simply tired. Hillsides short-grassed with hay stubble and alive with singing crickets offer only one or two yellow maple branches at their outer borders. Most of the inner leaves are still green. They hang limp and curling, a little discolored and discouraged at the edges. "Don't expect too much of us," they seem to say. "It's been a long year." Human, forgetful, with a touch of anticipated ice already chilling our imaginations, we take them at their word.

How can we be so foolish or forgetful? Every September we become victims of the same delusion, falling over and over again for one of Nature's best annual, regional jokes.

For there is no more glorious a seasonal phenomenon than autumn foliage in Vermont. And if I allow, grudgingly, that I may be biased—if I suppose, reluctantly, that there may be something, *somewhere*, that rivals in magnificence this Vermont transformation—still I see no reason to go looking for it. There is more than enough richness right here for one lifetime to absorb.

By the end of the month, not just one or two or a dozen, but every deciduous tree in the area has burst forth with spectacular color. The tiny poplar at the end of the driveway is as splendid as the giant maple in the front yard. Everywhere you look, some familiar, humble tree is beckoning in the most flagrant way. And by now, of course, everyone is pay-

ing attention. Doubts vanquished, forgotten or denied, we are all caught up by the season as it progresses, each in our own way keeping track of the nuances of color revealed by, the scientists tell us, the annual breakdown of chlorophyll in every dying leaf.

We are not so apt to document the process with scientific precision as we observe it. We applaud the presence of the bright yellow pigment (xanthophyll) as the birch leaves turn from green to pale gold; and the flashy performance of the compound carotene in each orange-yellow maple.

We share a running bulletin on the season as a whole, giving and receiving daily exchanges on its achievements in our particular area. Even the local newspapers and radio stations get into the spirit reporting foliage information with the same frequency and enthusiasm normally reserved for sporting events. "Barnet already shows good color," the announcer announces. "Danville is approaching peak." Whatever the claims of national and international news, Vermont radio stations always give air time to the leaves.

I have seen the foliage inspire even the most taciturn of citizens to hyperbole:

"This year, I think they've overdone it," a normally noncommittal neighbor allowed, breathing deeply as he took in the full scope of his view. In fact, the landscape spurs all of us to extra activity at this glorious moment of the year. This is the time when the axe and the chainsaw are busiest in the woodlot, when canning jars and freezer containers fill the counters in every kitchen, when children race and jump in piles of newly raked leaves, and in the barnyard even the animals catch the scent of the season. Young horses, fiery with the change in the air, career around the fence line, herding skittish sheep.

This is the season of foliage festivals. In our town, on "foliage day," local residents serve hot corn chowder and thick sandwiches on homemade bread to busloads of visitors, or dish up sugar-on-snow to those hardy individuals willing to climb the hill behind the town for dessert at an authentic Vermont sugar house. At night the corned-beef-and-cabbage dinner offers four successive sittings, and every year each one is sold out.

I am always amazed at the enthusiasm and good will engendered by this socializing, as well as the quantity of energy expended and the quantity of hot food consumed. True, the local people who work so hard on foliage day are making money for their churches, clubs or school organizations. But they are also making friends, many of whom return year after year to repeat the experience. The food shared is appreciated as enthusiastically as the landscape. Often a visitor will ask for a recipe for homemade pickles, or praise a particular delectable piece of pie, while at the same time admiring the foliage and the friendliness of the community. At the end of the day the local citizens, exhausted and beaming, are not sure what to treasure most.

All of this excitement seems somehow out of character. Where is our northern reticence, our famed reserve? In one quiet store in town, where the ladies behind the counter are so prim and polite that nobody speaks above a whisper, as if a sudden noise might disturb the china, two of them were raising their voices in blatant exclamation over the foliage.

"Well, how's the color out *your* way?" one woman asked me jubilantly, throwing off her customary reserve. The foliage does that to Vermonters. For a brief period every year, we are all a little unpredictable.

If you stop and think about it, even the New England landscape has an uncharacteristic look at this season. Suddenly colors of the South are running wild: hot oranges, deep red-to-purples, intense lemon-yellows. They have nothing to do with the quiet shades one normally expects from a cold climate. Their exuberance overwhelms the green decorum of the fir family, drenching the hills with light. Excess is the order of the season, although excess does not tally with our reputation at all. Perhaps, like poet Elinor Wylie when contemplating the exotic colors, sights and smells of the southern United States, we should confess in her bleak way:

Down to the Puritan marrow of my bones
There is something in this richness that I hate.
But we do not hate this richness of ours; we delight in it. For most of us, in fact, it has become indispensable to our annual inner balance, whether we recognize that or not.

"But it's almost *too* much!" protested a California friend who was here for the first time at the very peak of foliage season. Too much what? Too much to look at all at once? Too much frantic, disorganized color? Or is it simply too much for anyone from a warmer climate to understand a New Englander's love affair with this last, impossibly bright moment before winter? To her, our aesthetic sense at this season seems somewhat imbalanced. She does not

see that we are merely warming our hands and minds in preparation for the cold ahead.

Of course, there is no heat given off by this exercise except that which is kindled in our imaginations. It is odd that our images for autumn are so incendiary—"a blaze of color," "hillsides aflame," when in fact the weather at this time of year is closer to ice than fire. What really moves us, I believe, is not nature's simulated flames, or our brain's imagined warmth, not heat. It is light itself, revealed and reflected all around us in a multitude of ways. It touches everything from the softly backlit row of young beeches that line the country road we drive home on a September afternoon to the familiar, century-old maple that faces my desk outside a second-story window. This has always been a favorite tree, and now it displays a breathtaking array of leaves in several shades approaching yellow: leaves that are sun-colored, pumpkin-colored, lemon-colored, even peach-colored—a bursting tree full of light that fills the whole window. Underneath this vivid display I can see the careful, orderly, subdued dark network of branches. These too, so soon to be bare, look brittle, delicate, and lovely. These are autumn's bones.

Looking out this same window, I will notice in late October that the view is equally beautiful where there are leaves to admire and where the leaves have gone. By then my tree will be entirely stripped. It is one of the first to finish the cycle, its color consumed by wind and rain, sometimes, even by snow.

It is painful to see it go. It is not the thought of snow coming that gives a desolate note to the end of the season; it is the light leaving. For these two or three weeks our lives have been illuminated almost beyond belief by an extravagant celebration of light reaching beyond the merely decorative and into the human spirit. Autumn foliage leaves us with a vision of ineradicable beauty and we carry the vision with us through the winter. We may try to transmit it to others in letters, photographs, paintings, and spoken description, but we always lose a little in the retelling or reshowing. We lose even a little more during the passage of time, until the next Vermont autumn comes and we again call the foliage "unbelievable."

Perhaps this extraordinary annual offering that comes into our lives is most remarkable in that we did not earn it or ask for it. We cannot control it and we do not truly understand it. Who, after all, understands beauty on a grand scale? It is a gift unsought, and that in itself is astounding. Every year, unbelievably, this is for all of us—a gift of splendor, a gift of light.

A farmer and his cows, photographed by Richard W. Brown near Peacham.

The maples above hurl their flamed reflection to the windows of a house in Danby, photographed by Jim Eaton; ancient trees (left) arch against a feathered sky in South Newbury, by R.J. Alzner; a white horse (right) stands stark against the muted greens and yellows of a Northeast Kingdom forest, by Richard W. Brown.

91

The business of autumn is shown in these photographs: clockwise (right), the Old Meeting House in Strafford Village is the subject of the portrait by Hanson Carroll; playing in the leaves in Chelsea, by Peter Miller; a woman raking in Caledonia County, by Richard W. Brown; a band playing on the Grafton town green, by R. J. Alzner.

Autumn climaxes in breath-taking splendor, its brilliance surrounding
the town of East Topsham, left, VDA; above, two horseback riders
wind through the woods in Chelsea, by Peter Miller; a fiery orange
maple is photographed by Richard W. Brown in the Northeast Kingdom.

North Bennington's famed Old First Church, by Clyde H. Smith; a leaf-covered fountain in Waitsfield, photographed by William Hebden; right, mists rise above Granville Village, by Peter Miller.

A chill descends and the wind loses its softness. The rains fall.
We watch the leaves expire in their peak of color;
watch the mountains glaze. Autumn changes almost everything,
but in the change is offered the most promising of
messages; the circle will be unbroken. Vermont's autumn
changes will occur again, next year.

Late autumn on the Ottauquechee River in Bridgewater, by John Vachon.

Days of Grace

JOHN VACHON

It is that time of year, as an eminent sonneteer once put it, *when yellow leaves, or none, or few, do hang upon those boughs which shake against the cold....* It is after the fall; the color and splendor of autumn have vanished, and the last leaf watcher has driven back to Philadelphia. A scattering of snow can be seen at the top of Camel's Hump, but down below the land is brown and sere, the rivers run sparkling and unfrozen, and the first exuberant skier has not yet appeared at Stowe. It is early November; an equable quiet is in the air, and there's nobody here but us Vermonters. And me.

I have come back to this place that I've loved in all seasons, at a time when it is completely out of season. I want to see what Vermont looks like and to find out what Vermonters do after all the visitors go home: the bird watchers, the leaf lookers, the antique hunters, campers, arts and crafters, admirers of old houses and the summer theatre people. Now they have all gone away, and out-of-state license plates are as rare as picnickers or photographers. So, during these brief November days, I ramble the highways, side roads and back roads through the fourteen counties of the Free State of Vermont.

I find myself in an enchanting but unfamiliar landscape. There are no white church spires etched against vistas of hills in variegated greens, no town clocks to be seen through a gaudy spectrum of reds and yellows. Instead there is a soft and subtle pastel of tan and ochre, gray and lavender, with fine white lines drawn by birch trees in the hills. Town halls and churches blend unobtrusively into this quiet scene. A small sun that you can stare in the face is in the silent white sky, and the streams are molten lead. From its dark surface an unrippled lake reflects closed summer cottages and black tree tops, *where late the sweet birds sang.* A single leaf falls as a bird dips over the water. The fields and the woods and the banks of the Winooski are bare, and naked rocks protrude from the hills. A presentiment of winter is in the air, everywhere, but it is not sad, or even foreboding. It gets dark earlier now, and the lights in town go on at four o'clock. It rained a little this afternoon, and the streets are glistening. Plumes of smoke rise from chimneys, and there is a good smell of burning wood in town. A pumpkin-headed harvest figure sits slumped and neglected under a tree. But where is everybody?

Yesterday I saw a deer run across a front lawn in Shrewsbury. There were ruffled grouse in the woods, various warblers in the trees, ducks on the lakes and geese in the sky. But I saw few of my own species as I wandered through the towns and countryside. I saw no signs of rummage sales. I stood alone in the village green and wondered: are ancient plots of fiction being reenacted beneath that gabled roof? Is there anyone inside the Odd Fellows Hall? Or is someone watching me from the clock tower of the Congregational Church? There was no one at hand to answer my questions.

Eventually, I discovered that Vermonters are all alive and well this time of the year. They are enjoying these days of grace, and getting ready for the winter. The storm windows are mostly up by now. (Some of them were never taken down.) Snow fences have been unrolled and are standing in the fields, ready to balk the snow drifts. A few repairs must be made around the house on a Saturday afternoon: check the insulation of the basement, take down the front porch swing. A man in Duxbury touches up the red paint job on his closed barn door from which no horse has been stolen. A father watches his son tinker with the motor of the sputtering snowmobile, and remembers when he used to go on sleigh rides. A man named Brown in Chittenden County butchers a Hereford. That's food for the winter. A lady in Chelsea picks up fallen twigs from her front yard to use as kindling, and across the Common a man stacks up logs by his back door. Vermonters await winter calmly, and with no trepidation. They've handled it before.

It starts to get colder during Vermont's grace days. The kids come out to play in heavy red jackets and plaid wool lumberjack shirts, and they brighten up the landscape. On a Saturday morning, a twelve-year-old boy with a shotgun lopes down the road along a wooded river bank, his eyes searching for a partridge. An old man is raking up the few remaining decayed leaves that litter up his yard, and he fills the air with the blue smoke of their pungent burning. Late in the afternoon, the lights are turned on in Mills' Store, and sensible men sit around engaged in sensible conversation. "There's a feeling of snow in the air," one tells another. "It could come any day now." But not yet.

An unexpected surprise for anyone who travels during Vermont's days of amazing grace is the availability of gracious worldly comforts—good food and lodging. Most of my favorite village inns remain open. There are few guests, and reservations are hardly necessary. It is getting dark now, and I stop in front of an imposing porticoed mansion, set back from the street and designated "Tavern and Inn." Somehow there is a difference in the quality of welcome extended these days. Is it warmer, more personal? Perhaps it is because in November one is not a tourist. One is a traveler, passing through. A friendly lady shows me up a staircase to room number 8 on the second floor. She hands me a key, and now it is my room. There is a faint, pleasant smell of furniture polish. I cross over the wide floorboards to look out the window, stooping a little as the eaved ceiling gets lower. Out there the trees are swaying in the wind, and a boy on a bicycle hurries across the Green with a bag full of newspapers. Could the snow come tonight?

Downstairs a fine fire is blazing in a handsomely furnished room that doesn't deserve to be called the bar. A few other travelers are sitting there. I will go down and join them, pick up the *Brattleboro Reformer*, have a drink. We can talk, or not talk. Dinner is from seven to nine.

In the morning the sky is white and inscrutable; the snow is still holding off. It is a good day to stock up on maple syrup, apple cider and cheese. It's also a good day to visit some favorite bookshops, to examine some small town public libraries, to be the only visitor in a little museum.

Up in Adamant, in St. Albans, East Corinth and Troy, in Jericho and Chippenhook, Vermonters are scanning the skies beyond the birch and the beech in the hills, past the spruce and the fir on the upper slopes. They're not apprehensive, but they are ready. There is snow in the air today, and it won't be long now. It could come any time.

Quietly, unobtrusively, a few flakes will flutter down. And suddenly it will arrive in benevolent plenitude. Snow. All of Vermont will turn white, and everything will be "picturesque" again. Snow plows will clear the roads, and the chalets will open. There'll be skiers on the slopes and others mingling in the lodge. The ski tow will creak in the sparkling air, and weekenders will drink hot toddies. Pale faces from the city will grow ruddy by firelight, and daily Vermont snow conditions will be reported in *The New York Times*. Perhaps the old man in Bellows Falls will finally finish the *Pickwick Papers* this winter.

Burning leaves and a late afternoon, pick up game of soccer are seen in photographs by John Vachon. The Canada Geese, flying over the Dead Creek Wildlife Refuge in Addison, is by Clyde H. Smith.

In North Pomfret, stripped trees and empty fields stand ready for winter's invasion, photographed by R. J. Alzner; a stacked woodpile in West Topsham hints of the frigid weather to come, by John Belding.

*Sheep nibble the last green blades of grass, photographed in the
Northeast Kingdom by Richard W. Brown; a man prepares for
winter while there's still time, by John Vachon; a chill descends
on a cornfield in Pittsford, by Paul O. Boisvert.*

Darkening skies hang ominously over Enosburg Falls, photographed by Carolyn Bates; at right, Mt. Mansfield receives the first snows, photographed by Richard W. Brown; and a red-jacketed hunter, photographed by Carolyn Bates near Cambridge, lends the only bright color to a brown and white landscape.

In sudden drama, the late afternoon sun breaks through a dense cloud cover, by Carolyn Bates; an old barn in Barre Town stands in a frosted field, by John Belding; the last soft-pink rays of a sunset tinge the new snow cover outside Montgomery Center, by Carolyn Bates.

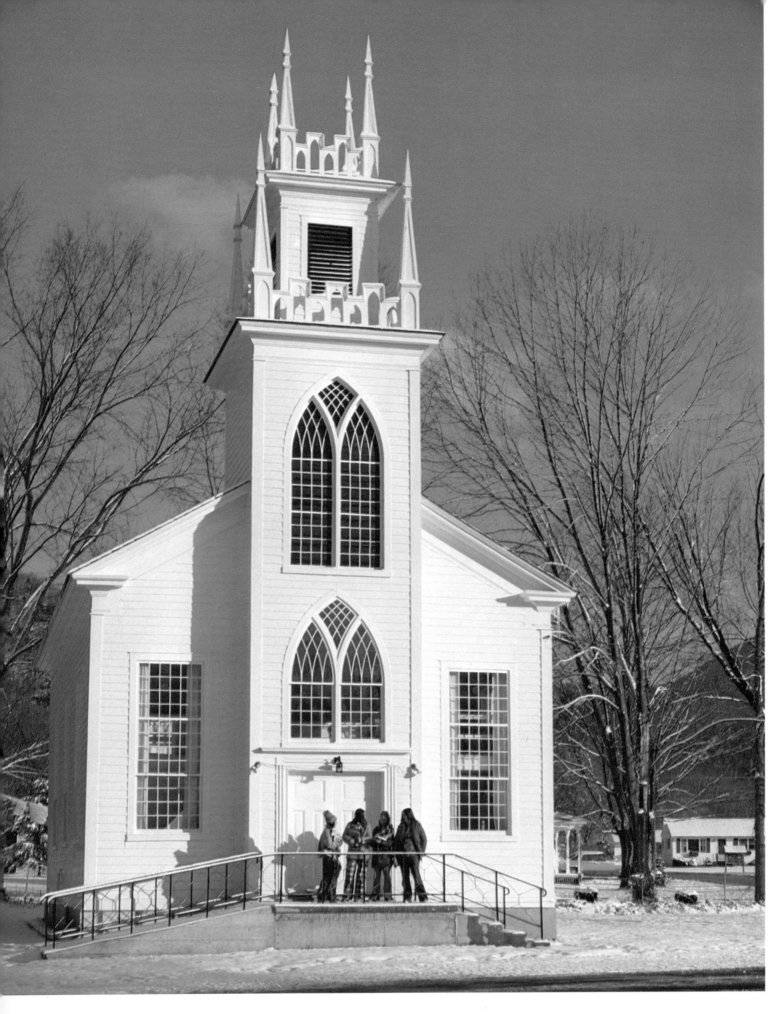

A church in Wells gleams against a bright blue sky, by Harold Rowe.

Days to Celebrate

RALPH NADING HILL

If a popularity poll were taken of the seasons, late fall and early winter might well vie for last place with mud-time. The sun has gone so far south and there's so little of it that in mid-afternoon it starts getting dark under the chairs. The hills and valleys are monotones of brown.

In this interval between rain and snow the only spectacle nature can manage that compares with spring's resplendent greens or autumn's blazing spectrum is to wrap every twig in an iridescent jacket. But let it warm up a degree or two and it disappears before you can get out your camera.

Most of the compensations in this drab hiatus between Thanksgiving and Christmas are internal. There is much to be said for being *forced* indoors after the last leaf has been raked, the last duck blind has been dismantled, deer rifles are back in their cases, the double windows are on, and the final guest has departed. (Whoever heard of a guest choosing to happen by in *this* season!)

Now at last you have time to clean out the closet, to restore some kind of order to your checkbook, return to the quilting frame, jigsaw puzzle, or the books you have only had time to dig into, or, if you've had your fill of football on television, just to sit and contemplate the state of the state or nation. It is my contention that the inventive prowess of early Vermonters had little to do with genes, but practically everything to do with being forced inside and to their own devices by the weather. There's no telling when the first snow will come or how long it will stay. When it does, it changes people's inner landscapes as completely as the out-of-doors, for it heralds the holiday season.

There have been years, though mercifully few, when it didn't snow, or what there was melted, and Vermont had a green Christmas. That is as much of a strain on the imagination as a white Christmas in Spanish moss country. In this northern climate the December law of averages is heavily weighted toward temperatures below 32 degrees, a leaden horizon gradually enveloping the whole sky, those first tentative flakes, and then a white curtain so dense you can hardly see the mailbox. If there is no wind and you happen to be in the fields or woods you can actually hear it snow. Within minutes everything that is not vertical—all those grays and browns from your feet to infinity—have turned dazzlingly white.

It is not in the least parochial to claim that the nation's ideal Christmas setting is New England, preferably Vermont with its yet unspoiled valleys and white villages. This durable vision portrayed long ago by Currier and Ives in their rural lithographs of holiday homecomings, conjures up a simpler world which decreed the family to be omnipotent and Christmas, particularly, to be a time of homecoming. It still is, of course, except that no one arrives by sleigh and it has been a long time since the atmosphere was pure of the ballyhoo of the commercial airwaves.

But the ancient message of Christmas is eternal, and the gathering of the clan, the time-honored tree, and exchange of presents have not changed. Among the other trappings of the season the most conspicuous has always been the kitchen with those wonderful aromas from the range: the turkey and ham, the bread, biscuits, and doughnuts, fruit cake, and plum pudding (though some of them may now come from stores down the street). Decades ago in the hinterlands the turkey and ham were domestic, that is to say, home-grown; the doughnuts came fresh and crispy from a hot kettle of lard, and the ice cream from a wooden-jacketed churn. Today's children who have never licked the dasher have missed one of life's prime delights. Then as now, of course, the Christmas tree in the church, the pageant of the Nativity, the wise men and shepherds tremblingly portrayed by the children of the parish with their gold paper stars, the bells outside, and the arrival of Santa Claus. These remain the ceremonies of a time to rejoice.

At least from a distance there is little other than electric lights and automobiles to distinguish the present from Christmases past. Snow lies deep over the same roofs it has for a century and a half; yellow light from the same windows streams across drifts covering the same pastures or lining the same streets or country roads. The tracks of the wild turkey have again joined those of the partridge, the snowshoe hare, the fox, and the deer; nothing in the woods has changed except that the forests have reclaimed so many of the mountain pastures of a century ago.

The popular conception of Vermont as the most rural state is true, so it is easy for strangers to overlook its cities. But, there again, most of their surroundings have survived, and where they have not, little violence has been done to what has replaced them, compared to the infestation of neon and commercialism so damaging elsewhere to the true spirit of the season.

It is a misconception to think that the mystique that surrounds the traditional Christmas in a rural setting has escaped those of us born and raised even in the state's largest city, with Lake Champlain at its doorstep and Mount Mansfield and Camel's Hump in its backyard. The same snow, though somewhat less of it, that blankets the mountains covers Burlington, and many of the same influences and associations affecting the rest of the state have always drifted into the lives of its people.

The early morning tinkle-bell of the horse that pulled a small wooden plow down the sidewalk is one of my own persistent memories of the city's first snowfall over five decades ago. School was out and a grand succession of free days stretched ahead until after New Year's. They didn't roll the snow in the streets as in smaller communities, they plowed them; but what was more important to children, they didn't scrape them bare. The hard-packed snow thus served the sleighs, of which there were still quite a few, and was suitable for automobiles—maybe one car every half hour or so on Route 7.

It had long been the custom to rope off Maple or one of the other streets descending steeply from the University to the harbor, and the traverses (long, narrow multi-passenger sleds with a front section that pivoted for steering, and a brake in the rear) attained legendary speeds. If the brakeman, exerting every ounce of strength to check the momentum of his 1000-pound cargo of people, could not stop, the sled continued past the docks onto the ice in the harbor, where at last it slowed to a halt.

For a long time there was a superb skating rink called Chiott's nestled between the wharves and separated from the harbor by a pile of snow. Nocturnal waterings with a long hose from the warming hut (in summer, a boathouse) which smelled of wet woolen mittens and hot dogs, kept the black ice flawless. On a cloudy Saturday afternoon with all the skaters' colored scarves, it looked like a painting by Brueghel.

The toboggan, much in evidence on the streets or steep icy slides built of staging to give you a good start, seems to have had its day. The jackjumper, a simple but tricky conveyance with a wooden seat and column fastened to a single runner, has almost passed from the scene, and the iceboats which streaked across the bays have been reduced to curiosities. During the last four decades the center of gravity has shifted to the mountains, where skiing has magnified the joys of descent a hundred-fold.

It is hard to be impersonal about the most intimate time of the year. Other than the Christmas morning I awoke to find strings of popcorn stretching from the head to the foot of my brass bed, my favorite recollection has to do with the old Rutland Railroad. Every loss is supposed to have its compensation, but nothing on rails can replace the steam locomotive, that thundering mass of metal that drew so many people away or brought them home. Since relatives did most of their arriving and departing at Christmas, the exhilaration of going to the station, listening for that far-off wail, and waiting for the tremulous yellow light and onrush of the engine's huge clanking drivers, its plumes of steam, and aroma of hot cylinder oil, is for me somehow all bound up with the holidays.

Intangibles of the spirit are hard to explain, and the Vermont mystique is particularly resistant to definition. It begins, I think, with a geography that makes large aggregations of people difficult or impossible. Other than in the state's few cities, its people are evenly spread throughout the valleys in small clusters which give them a sense of community, security, and independence. In the laps of mountains that "curl up in a coil," as Robert Frost observed, their villages became tiny principalities which have tended to insure the survival of the unalloyed democracy the founding fathers had in mind. And life in the Green Mountains guarantees an affinity with nature. Instead of people predominating over their environment, the surroundings prevail and human individuality is magnified against them.

Nor let us underestimate the variety and stimulation of the seasons, which impart the same qualities to the people. Anyone weaned on the seasons, at their most explicit this far north, cannot do without them, except perhaps when the mercury drops to twenty below.

But winter usually treats the Christmas season gently. It is wintry but not yet at its wintriest, and it belongs to the old year and not to the new. It is a time of its own, a time apart—a time to celebrate.

Snow-filled clouds loom over the Underhill Ski Bowl, by Dr.S. Henry Lampert; two sled-toting boys walk across the Green River Bridge in Guilford, by Michael McDermott; Richard W. Brown photographed these evening grosbeaks.

113

A home in Norwich stands distinctly against a cloudless sky, photographed by R. J. Alzner; the interior of the Old West Church in Calais is a study in simplicity, by Suzanne Opton; opposite, a moment of winter silence beneath Mt. Mansfield, photographed by Clyde H. Smith.

Opposite page and below, skiers at
Sugarbush take advantage of deep
powder, photographs by Clyde H. Smith;
the Ski Patrol on Prospect Mountain
in Woodford was photographed
by Carolyn Bates.

The moon above and lights below beam for weary skiers in this photograph by Richard W. Brown; Clyde H. Smith photographed the lazy (or crazy) window framing a storm outside and warmth and comfort inside.

In Brownsville farm buildings stand next to a narrow road made narrower by snowbanks, by Lee Wright; a farm in North Hero is prepared for the lowering temperatures of evening's onset, by Carolyn Bates.

After a day that has been crisp and clear and sunny, winter dusk moves in suddenly as photographed (left) on Lake Champlain in Shelburne by Paul O. Boisvert; above, skating in Strafford by DeWitt Jones; and, below, the evening rush hour in St. Johnsbury, by Richard W. Brown.

*The lights of the holidays shine brightly even past the deepest
snows and in the coldest temperatures, photographed by Clyde H. Smith
in Bradford (left), and in Lower Waterford.*

The thin ridge of dawn on the winter horizon exposes the grayish-pink early morning light, photographed by G. Allan Brown; a faded winter sun rises over Montpelier Junction (top right) by John Dowlin; and a sleigh ride in Stowe is photographed by Peter Miller.

Days for Digging Out...and Digging In

MARGUERITE WOLF

No one had prepared us for the little pleasures of living in the woods in winter. We were awash in dire predictions from non-Vermonters of deep snow, icy roads, power failures and frozen pipes. Even more gloomy was their predictable reaction when we said we planned to become "year-round summer folk."

"Oh, Vermont is beautiful, but how about the long winter? Won't you feel dreadfully isolated?"

City people, or even suburban folk—and we have been both—think of winter in terms of snow plowing and slick roads. So do we but they are *less* of a problem in the country. City streets are so clogged with parked cars and traffic that they are cleared very slowly and inadequately. Residential suburban streets are the last to be plowed because the town equipment is busy on the thoroughfares. We live one mile from the hard-topped road and that mile of gravel road—oh, all right, *dirt* road—is plowed right along with the hardtop because the big tank truck that bears the incongruous sign "Moo Juice Express" has to pick up our neighbor's milk from his dairy barn the same time every day. We have fewer days when the roads are slippery than we did when we lived in Westchester County, Boston or Kansas City because freezing rain is unusual here. When it gets cold it stays that way; none of this shilly-shallying around just above and below thirty-two degrees.

The real anxieties, and I admit there are a few in winter, are the possibility of a power failure and frozen pipes. We think about those because if our power was off for any length of time we would have no central heat, no running water, no electric light, no electric stove and no refrigerator. Now that's not as bad as it sounds. The wood stove would give enough heat for most weather. Water could be hauled from the spring. I've always loved candlelight. A refrigerator is redundant in the middle of winter and we could cook quite a lot on top of the wood stove and over the charcoal grill. But without the pump to keep the water moving in the pipes, they might freeze if it were below zero for an extended period of time. That's a remote possibility, hardly likely enough to warrant installing a

A steep and snowy hill is sanded in
North Pomfret, photographed by R. J. Alzner.

generator unless peace of mind has a higher priority than expense. The longest power failure we have ever experienced was not in Vermont but in Kansas City. When it is below zero we let the water run gently in the bathroom just to keep it moving through the pipes. Fortunately, our new well runneth over so we can afford to be a bit prodigal with water.

The other misfortune that is supposed to befall us is isolation. "You'll be so cut off from everything," we were told.

Being snowed in is a wonderful feeling, only it just doesn't happen. Once, years ago, when we lived in the country in South Burlington, we were snowed in for a day. George couldn't get to his office and the children couldn't get to school. I didn't hear much wailing or gnashing of teeth. It was a real holiday and the girls complained bitterly when our driveway was plowed and school reopened the next day. It is even less likely now because we have a snow blower. That wouldn't keep the schools open, but it takes about ten minutes to blow out the driveway and become mobile again. So being snowed in is a luxury we will probably have to forego.

But what nobody tells you is that winter in the country is a window of wildness, a time of seeing things as they really are and being a part of the drama of wildlife that comes right up to your door. There is no other season when you can tell just what has happened during the night. A deer mouse came out of the woods, crossed the deck, had a brief scuffle and dashed under the porch. A red squirrel jumped from the nearest pine tree, gleaned the seeds the chickadees had twitched off the feeder and ran back up the next pine tree. A deer came up our path from the brook, pawed at the straw covering our pipeline and moved on to the tastier hay banked around the house. Something startled it because it bounded away into an alder thicket in great leaps. If you turn on the deck light in the middle of the night you may look into the wide eyes and sooty twitching nose of a snowshoe hare two feet away. His big fluffy hind foot prints go all the way around the house and then back into the woods.

Regular visitors are the raccoons who stand on their hind legs and dig the bacon fat and peanut butter out of the holes in a bird-feeding log. They lick their fingers daintily and stare at you so curiously through their black masks that it is hard to remember how cross you are with them in the summer when they maraud the corn patch.

It frequently snows during the night, preparing an unmarked sheet for our human neighbors to transmit their news as well. I can tell if the mailman has come if his tire tracks have curved in towards the mailbox. One neighbor's daughter has been home for the weekend because her car's tracks are at the side of the house.

But while all this activity is informative, it is the silence of winter that hones the spirit. Thoreau said, "This stillness, solitude, wildness of nature is a kind of thoroughwort or boneset, to my intellect."

When I walk down the path to the brook, I hear only an occasional soft pluff as a pine bough unloads its burden of snow and bounds upward. The gurgle of the waterfall is muffled because it flows under another cascade of icefalls. The shape of the pool is constantly changing, sometimes almost all snow-covered with just an onyx eye of open water under the waterfall. There are tracks of small animals on the snow-covered ice where they have come to drink at the edge. Sometimes the pines are laden with snow and the slender white birches arc like girls with their heads bent down combing their long hair toward their bare toes. The rocks look like crouching polar bears and each fence post wears a fat marshmallow on top. A house or barn that I had never noticed before emerges when the leaves have fallen.

The distinctive wine glass shape of an elm, the widespread craggy arms of an oak or the gnarled cupped hands of an apple tree label the species more clearly at a distance than if they were in leaf. And I have been surprised this winter at the amount of color in what we think of as the muted season. The osiers are crimson and there is frosted purple bloom on the black raspberry canes. The various browns of the weeds and ferns poking up out of the snow have the mellow warmth of wood tones, chestnut, mahogany and pale ash. Weeping willows glow even in winter and the apple twigs have a rosy sheen. Winter sunsets are citrus colored, tangerine, pale lime and lemon. The same golden and pale wash of green are reflected on the breasts of the evening grosbeaks splitting open sunflower seeds on our feeder. Tiny rainbows sparkle everywhere on the surface of new snow and in the distance the mountains turn from blue to rosy purple in the late afternoon.

After a storm the meadows are seas of white, drifted and swirled into waves that crest and throw off a spume of fine snow.

We enjoy people and need them but even more we need and enjoy this feeling of being insulated against the jackhammers of noise and crowds. More than three hundred years ago John Donne wrote, "No man is an island, entire of itself." That is still true, but it has become even more true that every man yearns for an island, a place where he can be surrounded by whatever nourishes his individual spirit. Perhaps some people can find their island within the city and get their nourishment from the constant stimulation of all of their senses. But I prefer the natural colors of a sunset to neon lights, the chuckling of our brook to pneumatic drills, the taste of apple pie to French pastry, the smell of arbutus to exhaust fumes and space around me instead of bodies in the subway. I like islands, frames of quiet or distance, to set off the notes of a hermit thrush or a snow-capped mountain.

It is all very simple and goes way back to Antaeus, who was the child of the sea, as we all once were. He became stronger when he touched the earth. And so do we.

*Relaxing near the warmth of a wood stove, by G. Allan Brown;
the setting sun casts long shadows as three walkers stroll
to their Arlington home, by Carolyn Bates.*

It usually comes in February, and for reasons not altogether
logical, it usually begins in the late afternoon.
By nightfall, its intent is well known and only its force
and impact have to be guessed at. The weather,
its variety and extremes, is any Vermonter's conversation
piece at every season.

*Digging out in Randolph, by Marjorie Ryerson; snowblowing by Lois Moulton.
Against a backdrop of the Meeting House in Strafford, right, a couple
engages in winter exercise, photographed by Hanson Carroll; the woman above
shovels out from under a record snow storm in Cavendish, by Helen Holland.*

130

Arctic winds blow around a house in Johnson, photographed by Clyde H. Smith;
in the Northeast Kingdom, wood smoke sends plumes into the freezing morning air,
by Richard W. Brown. Opposite; winter snow and plunging temperatures do not
completely stop work at the granite quarries in Barre, by John Belding;
smoke punctuates the skyline in Stowe, photographed by Clyde H. Smith.

133

A townscape in Bethel (left) is seen through the fragile frame of
a Victorian door, photographed by Lud Munchmeyer. A frosted forest
stands above a Northeast Kingdom farm, by Richard W. Brown.

In winter the Vermont barn is a greenhouse for the animals,
a Yankee oasis in a severely hostile climate,
a domesticated Noah's ark solidly anchored
in a five-month flood of snow.

In the warmth of a winter barn, a farmer feeds a hungry calf as a
curious cat hovers waiting its turn, and opposite, a smooth sheet of
new snow reflects the cloudless blue sky on this Caledonia
County farm, photographed by Richard W. Brown.

A Day of Ice

J. DUNCAN CAMPBELL

Quietly in the night, things change. But only those who are still awake can suspect anything. Snuggling under quilts, they hear the faintest whisper of some new kind of precipitation. Outside, unmarked fields in every direction are being coated with diamonds.

By morning, everything has been encased. Each twig on every tree can be seen through the ice and the sun glares from its surfaces as from a mirror. There is no form too intricate to be coated, from the tops of the highest trees to the most glittering rocks at stream side.

The world is slippery. Yet, in between the villages and towns, the main paved roads are already salted and sanded. The trucks are still crawling quietly along, lights flashing, as daylight blends with the glow of their headlights along the snowy ice-crusted ditches and fields.

Early investigators—the Vermont cats—fastidiously inspect the surface with tentative paws while an occasional, unwary dog slides inexorably backwards down some gleaming slope while scrambling madly in the other direction.

Highly crowned, smooth gravel side roads are impassable for any but those intrepid Vermonters who steer with finger tips, body English, and transcendent skill. Kitchen radios at breakfast recite the school bus runs that have been cancelled.

Youngsters rush to get out their sleds—flexible flyers for the purists, red plastic sheets for the more contemporary and garbage can lids, cardboard boxes or the tops of TV trays for the improvisational. This is a time when you can coast forever.

The middle of the long hill driveway is raised and stones poke up through the ice, making fair traction for winter boots. But the sides of the driveway are as smooth as smooth from the broad wheel tracks and children who have hiked to the top now turn, grasping their sleds across their chests, and belly-flop expertly into one wheel track or the other. How quickly the sleds respond! Coasting on soft snow is *nothing* compared with this. Down and down again the sledders go, cheating at the very last by pushing like crabs and finally, reluctantly, coming to a full stop.

Cross country skiers know that the easy snow conditions of the past few hours were only loaned. Now, in the late afternoon, scudding clouds come rolling over the dark blue ridges to the west. The temperature is falling and raindrops begin to sting their ears, then bounce slightly as they strike the snow. The tracks they made to reach the place they stand in are being obliterated. But then suddenly, as will happen on these days of ice, the temperature plummets to twenty degrees and those tracks freeze into impossible, solid ridges. Ice as strong as steel on the ground, as transparent as glass and as fragile as breath in the trees.

The next morning, the alpine skier is out early. His first run had been dangerous, quickly exhausting, in a chilling wind. Now the sun is warmer and as the skier prepares for another run, he senses something. He stops, glancing around and then up. The sky has changed and is now a deeper blue. But that isn't it, he decides. He sniffs the air. No new smell. Just air, so clean and cold that it has no flavor.

He listens. The mountain is quiet. But he can faintly hear the clack-clacking of the ski lift and he can pick up the sound of a truck laboring, far down the mountain. But there is something else. What is it?

The skier slumps over his poles and stares off across Vermont from his high perch. Then the message begins to arrive again and it ripples up his back and plucks notes somewhere in his head. It's music, that's what it is. A trillion tiny ice-encrusted chandeliers responding to being struck by bits of ice melted off twigs above. All around him, and for as far out as he can see, branches are slowly bending, shivering, springing up again. Branches below are being immersed in glittering blizzards of ice from above. All this sifting downward through the most unthinkably complicated of instruments.

Strange that a harp of thousand strings
Should stay in tune so long.

Joyfully, the skier pushes upward from both poles. The skis flash in the sun as they arc, together, downward to the left, crunching softly now and in perfect tune with the orchestral arrangement of ice that is playing all around.

An iced willow tree near Bradford,
photographed by Winston Pote.

An ice-encrusted landscape sparkles in the afternoon sun, photographed by Hans Wendler in Corinth.

140

Days of Maples and Mud

NANCY PRICE GRAFF

There is something unpleasant about a month that comes and overstays its welcome. Like the guest who comes to dinner and stays on long after the fires have been banked and the welcome mat has been pulled back across the threshold, it is guilty of a breach of etiquette. The affront, of course, is a seasonal rather than a social one, but it is no less real or forgivable. March is such a month.

Derived from the latin "mars" for martial, "March" is clearly a misnomer. No other month has such leaden feet or such a weak sense of purpose. At a time when most of us would welcome a quick, short fight and a hasty surrender to warmth, March launches a flurry of ineffective but annoying counteroffenses against the coming of spring. It leads us through a series of retreats from the heat of battle with the new season.

March's greatest sin, however, has nothing whatever to do with overstaying its welcome or dragging its feet. It has to do with mud. Anyone who has watched the ground thaw and the world sink to its knees in March knows that mud is the nub and nemesis of the season. During this hiatus in the annual cycle, mother earth goes soft in the core and reneges on her responsibility to keep a firm footing under things. Mud transforms the merest slivers of open space into quagmires and the roads to dance floors. It accumulates on my doorstep, refuses to be content in the room I have named in its honor, and runs rampant through the house. Like Dr. Seuss' insidious green stain, it is everywhere, a contagion without a cure.

This untidiness is at the heart of my objection to the 31 days that stretch between the end of February and April Fool's Day. Snow that fell like a lush shag carpet in the middle of winter wears to a thin, bedraggled mat that no amount of halfhearted dusting will improve and that no respectable housekeeper would tolerate for a minute. The world washes to a uniform brown and low-hanging clouds snap in the corners of the sky like cobwebs just beyond the poke of a mop handle. Thick and ominous, the clouds become a moist web, ensnarling our heads and thoughts.

There might still be room in my heart for this

Winter begins to slip away from this Barnet farmscape, by Richard W. Brown.

morass that calls itself a month if these were isolated faults, but the curmudgeonly drummer who beats for March carries all of us along. Car batteries that have kept their charge through three frigid months, faithfully leaping at the simple turning of a key, lose their vigor and gag frightfully before expiring altogether. Neighbors eye each other warily across their spent woodpiles, suspicious that the five cords they labored to stack last October should have dwindled so rapidly or threaten so ominously to give out entirely and leave the laborers cold and friendless. Crocuses, coaxed to push their colorful heads through the melting snow cover at the first false signs of spring, are frozen in the bud.

Even winter's cure takes its cue from March's derivation and rides roughshod over us. The wind that comes to escort the season out the door quickly swells from a slight stir among stiff branches to a steady gale. It frees the detritus trapped by winter's snow and whips it about our ankles and into our eyes. Tender branches that have withstood blizzards snap off at the joint and shower down upon us like feebly tossed darts. The wind whistles by our ears, stings our eyes, rumples our hair, lifts our skirts, tears at our coats, and eventually tightens the muscles in our jaws.

In this mood we are called together on the first Tuesday of the month for our appointed democratic exercise. This annual ritual of assembling to learn the town's business (and everyone else's) could hardly come at a less propitious time. Heaving roads, abuse of salt, and mailboxes flattened by wayward plows too often dominate discussions that if convened at a more pleasant time of the year would, in all probability, be more rapidly concluded. Granted, some of the town's more important business matters might be given bare consideration were more inviting temperatures competing for our time outdoors, but is that any reason to hold Town Meeting Day in early March? Well, perhaps it is.

Luckily, at this moment when we are all at our most disagreeable, nature waits for no man. Maple trees whose twiggy tops have long been all ears to the sounds of coming spring and whose deeply rooted feet felt the earth's thaw long before the rest of us sensed the softness underfoot, let loose their sap to drip into buckets hung from their trunks.

During this first stretch of warmer days, sugaring is the swift kick in the seat of our senses that sets us once again in motion. We feel our own blood begin to move at this sign of nature's pulse. Our hopes for the new spring swell in the smoke billowing from sugarhouses and a thousand winter sins are forgiven in a moment.

At these times it is easy to see the promise in the sun's longer arc across the sky. Children dart from the house without their parkas to test the air. Neighbors pause on the sidewalk in snatches of sun to renew friendships. Windows are thrown open to freshen rooms gone stale by winter's long visit and rugs on the line are beaten to shake loose the sawdust that accumulates in front of the woodstove. Crocuses now successfully burrow up through the mulch to try their colors.

Perhaps if March fell at another time of the year it would not seem so great a test of our patience. Unhappily for it and us, however, March is stuck between a rock and a soft place. It rarely shows to good advantage; it's simply something to be gotten through on the way to painting birdhouses, planting seeds, lambing sheep, and spring cleaning.

Fortunately, March does pass. Like the guest who comes to dinner and finally finds the manners to take his leave, March, too, eventually makes its exit. Sometime around the end of the last week, without a moment to spare, it tires of its procrastinating games and finds its way. A stronger sun than we have felt or seen in four months reduces the last scraps of snow to shallow puddles and begins to dry the ground for spring planting. The wind that has been throwing such heavy punches, gentles, and at the eleventh hour, finally ushers in a new sweet-smelling season.

The snows begin to melt and the sap begins to flow in Union Village, by Hanson Carroll; at right, a sugarhouse in Pomfret, by Clyde H. Smith; boiling sap in Elmore, VDA.

When the cold, sharp winds of March mingle
with the warming sun of coming spring, Vermont towns
set aside the first Tuesday of the month for a
day of self government, where a cross section of people
who make direct democracy work, have a chance
to make themselves and their ideas heard.

On the first Tuesday in March,
photographs by Richard W. Brown.

March will occasionally leave like a lion in the Connecticut River Valley, photographs by Richard W. Brown. Opposite, gathering sap in Shelburne, by Paul O. Boisvert.

This is the time of year when the earth seems to hang in
a precarious balance between the two most opposite seasons;
it is easy to forget that one last inevitable storm will come.
Then the last snow of real consequence occurs, making an emphatic
flourish of winter's departure. It is winter's annual rite
of passage, that final exiting exclamation point.

Early spring is disguised in white but baby lambs, sheep and children sense its imminent arrival, as photographed by George C. Wilson (top left), Richard W. Brown (bottom left) and in Randolph by Marjorie Ryerson (above).

Somewhere between the time winter tips its hat
to spring and the day of spring's true arrival
is a period of weeks called mud season.

The sun frees the ground of frost, photographed by C. A. Murray in Hartland, left, and, right, by DeWitt Jones in Thetford.

Afterword

GEORGE D. AIKEN

In his Introduction to this volume Charles Morrissey says,"The yearly cycle in Vermont is a refresher course." How true that is! I've been taking that "refresher course" for more than eighty years now—ever since as a youngster I would walk into the woods bordering my father's farm on Putney Mountain and find a good tree stump to sit on. I'd watch, and listen, and think. Looking around at countless species of plant and animal life I could get an understanding of the works of nature which probably I would never have learned in a lecture hall in college or a legislative hall in Montpelier or Washington. Each year I refresh my knowledge of what I've learned since growing up in Vermont— and reconfirm that nature has surprising lessons to teach us if we will pay attention.

Take the morning of March 20 as an example. This is the first day of spring, says the calendar, but icicles from the eaves may be two feet long. Are these wintry icons a proper greeting for spring? Well, a Vermonter won't feel cheated by the weather if he has put taps on a few hundred maple trees—or only on a half-dozen trees near home. Those icicles could predict the best run of maple sap of the season, assuming of course that March 21 would be a nice day with the temperature varying from 45 to 55 degrees Fahrenheit and the wind would be soft and westerly.

As a youngster in Putney I would usually tap a couple of trees near the house. Five-pound lard pails were used as sap buckets while spouts were whittled from the branches of nearby sumachs. The spouts were three or four inches long with the pith burned out of them by a wire croquet wicket heated red hot in my mother's cookstove. As soon as a couple of quarts of sap could be gathered I would start boiling it down on the cookstove until a half-cup or more of tasty syrup would remain. The quality of this kitchen product might not rate as "Fancy," or "Grade A," or even "Grade B" as required by the marketing rules of the 1980's, but it tasted real delicious—especially if boiled down enough to be eaten as "sugar on snow." The snow would be collected from the last drifts of winter. In my boyhood nobody complained about snowdrifts or ici-

cles on the first day of spring if the promise of homemade maple syrup was in the air.

The first of April was also a special day for us. Nature might play the biggest April Fool's joke on us by dumping a foot of wet snow, but in the village the storekeepers, and other suppliers of farm equipment and the like, very much had the spring market on their minds. Merchants would inventory their goods on April 1st because everything on hand was subject to local taxation. On April 2nd they would start to restock by ordering items which they noted on April 1st were in low supply.

April 1st was also important to a lad in the early 1900's because then it was only thirty days before the opening of the trout fishing season. From that day onward I would count the days of waiting—29, 28, 27, and so forth—until the waiting was over. My fishing pole was usually cut from a black birch tree growing in a grove of saplings. The fish line was cut from the hardest twine available, and fish hooks were bought at the local store for two cents each. Fish worms for bait were dug from the ground at the end of the short drain from the kitchen sink (where we also raised horseradish). At daylight on May 1st I was eager to go down to the brook less than half-a-mile away.

No trout under six inches in length could be legally brought home but, sad to say, some Putney boys of eighty years ago felt the law could be bent as easily as a supple fishing pole. They would build a small bonfire, cut a pointed stick on which to fasten the short trout, and cook them over the flames. They never told their mothers about this when they got home.

The brook at the foot of our field had a great attraction. Besides fishing we would swim there— with or without bathing suits—throughout the summer. One time I met up with an old mud turtle at our swimming hole. Never having met a snapping turtle before, I punched at it with a stick. The turtle took up the challenge. He grabbed the stick and wouldn't let go. With the stick over my shoulder and the turtle hanging on for dear life I carried him all the way back home before we called a truce and I put him down. This turtle, like all members of the species, knew how to follow directions without a compass. He circled a couple of times and then started on a straight beeline for his home in the brook a half-mile away. I still wonder

Mt. Mansfield displays a persistent chilly face, but the bare fields announce a new season, by Richard Howard.

why bees and turtles share such an unerring sense of direction.

The first of May was most important for another reason. That day was earmarked for hanging May baskets, and both boys and girls used them to express their more-than-casual affection for a young person of the opposite sex. The May baskets were usually handmade and often held a couple of pieces of candy bought for a few cents at the village store in addition to a bouquet of native wildflowers. We picked spring beauties, bloodroot, hepatica, dutchman's breeches, and others which bloom at that time. Under the rules, if a boy found a May basket for him on the family doorstep he could catch and kiss the young lady who left it there. The same rules applied if a girl found a May basket. In the schoolyard I noticed that boys could often run faster than girls, but after leaving a May basket the boys seemed to lose that swiftness.

Spring was the most important season for all members of the family; what we did then would determine our income later in the year. After washing and storing the sap buckets, holding tanks and the evaporator, we mended fences, rebuilt stonewalls, and cut wood which would dry in the warm weather for use as fuel the following winter. Spring plowing with oxen or horses would prepare the soil for sowing oats or grass seed. In those days an acre a day was considered good plowing; today, with a $15,000 tractor and a four-bladed plow, an acre an hour is not too much to expect.

We would sow seeds indoors in the spring. After mid-March the sunlight coming through the windows of the parlor and the sitting room would furnish what today we call solar energy. This heat would nurture the seedlings of cabbage, tomatoes, and other vegetables which would later be transplanted in the garden. The first of nature's contributions to our dinner table was dandelion greens, followed by cowslips, milkweed, and fiddleheads. By late June we had picked early peas, enjoyed the new growth of asparagus, and welcomed fresh lettuce, radishes, and spinach.

Summer weather brought crops of wild and cultivated fruits and berries, providing delicious food for the daily table and also jams and jellies for the cold months to follow. Strawberries were the first of the cultivated berry crops to ripen; we would pick them from mid-June until mid-July. They became one of the major fascinations of my life. In 1930, I received the first patent rights ever granted in the United States for an ever-bearing strawberry. Being a Vermonter I named this variety the Green Mountain Strawberry. By the outset of World War II over a million of these plants had been sold. If I hadn't

been busy in the U.S. Senate for 34 years, and busy teaching at the University of Vermont and doing an oral history with Charlie Morrissey when I retired to Vermont in 1975, I probably could have developed some more varieties of strawberries by now.

Summer in my boyhood was a busy season, too, but not without its time for fun. We often fished on rainy days and after work at night. The Connecticut River enticed me down from the mountain whenever I could get a chance, and we fished for perch, walleyed pike, black bass, and hornpouts. The latter, which we called bullheads, were really a species of catfish and would sleep by day but swim about at night. At a favorite spot below the Putney railroad station we often had good luck. One night I caught several big ones, some twelve to fifteen inches long, when my line hooked what seemed like a whopper. When I finally landed it I discovered I had hooked a sack of stable manure. Somebody who knew a favorite diet of hornpout had thrown it into the river a few days before. After I raised the sack the fish would bite no more that night. Tossing a sack of manure into the Connecticut River would strike us today, with our stringent environmental laws, as an unsound practice. But the fish didn't seem to mind—nor did we when we ate them.

In late August the sweetcorn is ready to harvest—at least it is for some folks. To be honest, although I have planted sweet corn for several recent years, we haven't had a dozen good ears for our own table. That funny-faced fellow called a raccoon by some, and less complimentary names by others, keeps track of my corn from the time it breaks the ground in the spring until it is about ready to be picked. Each year I think I will get the best of him and pick it all some morning whether it is quite ready or not. But I just can't win. Mr. Funny Face seems to know just when I plan to pick it, and inevitably the night before he brings his wife and three children to harvest every ear. In the morning I give myself another zero rating for thinking I can outsmart one of the shrewdest inhabitants of the forest. The skunks also like sweet corn, but they pay something for it by keeping the moles and other garden pests under control.

Before August is over other garden crops are being harvested—cucumbers, tomatoes, cauliflower, carrots, and if the soil is sandy or gravelly enough we pick watermelons and cantaloupes. These are pint-sized varieties and not as good as the old-fashioned kinds we used to grow. At one time I raised 27 varieties of melons for the U.S. Department of Agriculture but I doubt if any of these are grown in Vermont today.

All summer we can pick raspberries—red, black, yellow and purple. If the autumn is gentle they may be available from new varieties until October. Cultivated blueberries now are also available from early July until late September. On warm August days we pick peaches, pears, plums, and quinces, but after nightfall, when the northern lights glitter in the sky above us to the northeast, it is evident that autumn is upon us. Very little work got done on Labor Day when I was a youngster, but significantly we went to bed early that night. Fall chores began in earnest on the day after Labor Day.

My father grew tobacco and sold the leaves for cigar wrappings, and in early September we cut the last of that crop and hung it in the top of the barn to dry. Our neighbors who kept cows would try to get a third cutting of clover or alfalfa and also start filling the silo. Picking apples and digging potatoes were underway by mid-September and continued until mid-November. Those were the days when potato fields of several acres were common, and freight cars would be filled with them at railroad stations and carried to the cities. Sizeable crops in northern Vermont were shipped to Florida and planted there soon after arrival. The following spring the new crop would be shipped back to northern markets. Today the potato business isn't what it used to be in Vermont; people now want potatoes in the form of chips, sticks, and French fries, but I still get a thrill from digging up a two-pounder in my own garden.

Apple orchards aren't what they used to be, either. In my youth a farmer might maintain 30 to 50 trees, but today an orchard of 200 acres or more is considered to be practical in size. No longer do we collect empty flour barrels from the country stores to ship apples to New York or Boston. Nor do we let sheep into the orchard in order to eat wormy apples which have fallen to the ground. In my father's modest orchard I learned to admire black snakes because they were helpful in controlling the mouse population.

Wormy apples had their uses, however; they made cider which was just as good as cider from the sounder ones. And good cider made in the fall, if held in its natural condition until the next summer when it became hard cider, made it easier to hire help for haying. It was worthwhile to have a happy haying crew because we mowed much of the hay with hand scythes, gathered it with horses or oxen, and used pitchforks to toss it to the scaffolds of the barn.

In the autumn we felt we were working against time, but still we paused to enjoy the colorful foliage and happy occasions like husking bees. On an evening in mid-October a farmer and his neighbors might husk a hundred bushels or more of corn to feed to his livestock through the upcoming winter. Most of this corn was an eight-rowed flint corn, yellow in color, but from time to time somebody would husk a bright red ear. Any boy who found a "red ear" was entitled to kiss any girl at the bee. Some folks say the boys secretly brought red ears with them in order to liven up the evening.

Not long after the corn and apples were picked we would plan for Halloween. The clergy and high-minded citizens of Putney tried to maintain a proper decorum among the youth of our community, but it was not unusual for the minister to find that a sheep or calf had been lifted into the church belfry, or that church bells would chime at unholy hours. One Halloween a neighbor had driven to the village and imbibed too freely; on the journey homeward, three miles long, he wondered why the hill seemed so steep. Finally he realized that village pranksters had switched the small wheels on the front of his buckboard to the rear, and the large rear wheels to the front, and that was why the hill seemed steeper on Halloween.

November at last: the brilliant autumn leaves were mostly on the ground, the corn was in its crib, the hay in the barn, and the apples in the cellar. Before Thanksgiving the pig had to be slaughtered and hung from a branch of the big maple tree. It had been bought as a piglet in the spring for three or four dollars and fed table scraps by my mother until it got to be a regular member of the family (and the biggest member of the family too, weighing over 200 pounds). I used to hide under the bed until the squealing had ended and my father had completed the job. My mother would never eat any part of the pig which she had fed all summer and which trusted her.

The pig was not the only sacrifice for Thanksgiving. The Plymouth Rock rooster bought in the spring to make sure the hens laid fertile eggs had to pay his price, too. The day before Thanksgiving the rooster's head would be laid on the chopping block.

But Thanksgiving was really a joyful day. Families which hadn't seen each other for months got together. Some years there was snow on the ground by Thanksgiving, and the ice was thick enough on the pond for skating. In other years the autumn has persisted deceptively; on December 2nd in 1979 I picked a bushel of sound apples, and the earth was brown for most of the winter which ended March 19, 1980. As a youngster, however, we always cleaned the sawdust out of the icehouse before Christmas and readied our ice plow, ice saw, ice tongs and weatherproof clothing. On the day after

Christmas we would start cutting ice which was usually eight inches thick on the local pond, and by the first of January it would, in a normal winter, be a foot thick. I fell into the ice pond one winter day when it was 20 degrees below zero; I ran full-speed to home, a quarter-mile away, and my clothes were frozen stiff before I got there. The memory of that still makes me shiver.

We cut ice into blocks which were eighteen inches square; packed in sawdust they would survive in the icehouse until the last of the hot days of the following summer. A huge ice house near Putney station stored hundreds of tons of ice cut on the Connecticut River, and that cooled the milk shipped by rail to Boston.

Christmas Eve was celebrated in our one-room schoolhouse with a spruce tree cut from up on the mountain and decorated by strings of popcorn and real wax candles. Presents were largely handmade and even Christmas ribbon candy was not plentiful. A real pleasure was chocolates bought for twenty cents per pound. I would usually get a comb for my mother; if I were lucky I'd get a jackknife. The important thing about Christmas, though, was the spirit. For the hope of the human race, I hope this never dies.

We did logging in the winter because it is easier to skid logs out of the woods when snow covered the ground. For recreation we relied on a home-made toboggan, and when the snow was crusty we slid on dish pans or scoop shovels. Surprisingly, I remember New Year's Day as just another work day. But Town Meeting Day, in early March, was festive because it brought the community together as winter began to relent. Despite the fact that town meetings in Vermont are not the medium of local government they used to be, they still are the nearest form to government by the people to be found. I treasure town meeting so much that I would come home to Putney from Washington when I was in the U.S. Senate in order to serve as town moderator. I'd rather be on the floor of the town hall than on the floor of the Senate chamber on the first Tuesday after the first Monday in March. Besides, right after town meeting, at my home on Putney Mountain, I could think about tapping those maple trees, and ruminate about the lad who once went into the woods to sit on a tree stump and learn about nature.

Today, as I look from our porch across the hills and forests of Vermont, I understand why so many good people from other states have bought land near our home and hope to build their own homes and settle here as soon as circumstances permit. Being in touch with the changing seasons of Vermont, and knowing what nature can reveal to us, is a rich experience. Often I think to myself, "Thank goodness I was born and raised in Vermont." This is my home and always will be.

Contributing essayists to this volume share one very important trait in common: they all reside in Vermont. Aside from that commonality, and a shared affection for their home that is more than merely suggested in their words, they are as diverse as the Green Mountain State itself.

Charles T. Morrissey, consulting editor and author of the introduction, is a Montpelier resident, adjunct professor at the University of Vermont, former director of the Vermont Historical Society and a nationally known oral history consultant. His major subject in recent years has been **George D. Aiken** of Putney, author of this volume's afterword.

Governor Aiken has spent six decades in public service in Vermont, including terms as Lieutenant Governor, Governor and 34 years as U.S. Senator. Originally a successful orchardist and cultivator of wild flowers by profession, he is author of *Pioneering with Wildflowers* and *Senate Diary.*

Donna Fitch writes lovingly of the state she knows so well, having been raised on a farm in Calais, Vermont. Her observations of bringing a harvest home have a ring of authenticity because she knows of harvesting from firsthand experience. She is a free-lance writer whose additional contributions to this volume include research and captions.

Ronald Rood, well-known naturalist and long-time resident of Lincoln Vermont, is the author of *How Do You Spank a Porcupine!* and *It's Going to Sting Me: A Coward's Guide to the Great Outdoors,* plus some ten other books.

Mildewed letters, uncovered while remodeling an old house in Jericho, Vermont, initiated **Marguerite Wolf'**s writing career— from history to essays. Some of her book titles include *How to Be a Doctor's Wife Without Really Dying* and *Sheep's in the Meadow, Raccoon's in the Corn.*

Ralph Nading Hill, a Senior Editor of *Vermont Life* magazine, is a renowned historian and author of many books about the north country including *Lake Champlain: Key to Liberty, Yankee Kingdom, Contrary Country,* and *The Voyages of Brian Seaworthy,* (a novel). He lives in Burlington where he was born.

Nancy Price Graff lives in Montpelier, is a graduate of Middlebury College, and wrote a history of that community, *At Home in Vermont.* Now her writing encompasses a wider area and she contributes to several publications, including *Vermont Life.*

Reeve Brown, teacher, wife and mother, writes of her adopted state from the Barnet farm where she and her photographer husband, Richard W. Brown, live. She is also a free-lance writer.

J. Duncan Campbell moved to Vermont from Brooklyn, New York 35 years ago and counts it among his most important decisions. He is a Senior Editor of *Vermont Life,* a selectman in the town of Bennington and an industrial designer and businessman.

Anne O'Leary is a free-lance writer living in Southern Vermont and is attending Vermont Law School in South Royalton.

John Vachon, who wrote "Days of Grace" shortly before his death in 1975, was a would-be Vermonter who would visit the state on almost any pretext. He was a professional photographer for 40 years but fancied himself a writer as well. Many thought that dual distinction was justified, including his son.

—Brian Vachon